Franchising Your Business

Franchising Your Business

An Owner's Guide To Franchising As A Growth Option

By Donald D. Boroian and L. Patrick Callaway

FRANCHISING YOUR BUSINESS
A Francorp Publication

ISBN: 978-0-9816488-0-4

Francorp, Inc.
20200 Governors Drive
Olympia Fields, IL 60461
708-481-2900
800-372-6244
www.francorp.com

Francorp Staff:
Chairman: Donald D. Boroian
President: L. Patrick Callaway
Project Editor: Richard Gosswiller

Printed in the United States of America

To all the exciting, dynamic entrepreneurs we have known.

Acknowledgement

Our special appreciation to Richard Gosswiller, who edited this and our previous two books. As a lifelong friend and former Senior Vice President of Francorp, he brought something very special to this book which could not have been done without him.

Thanks Dick,
The Authors

Contents

■■■■

Introduction

■ ■ ■ ■

In our first book, *The Franchise Advantage*, published in 1987, we attempted to broadly describe the franchise phenomenon, including its history and its impact upon the American economy and economies around the world. In it we predicted that "franchising will make the world smaller." Thomas Friedman came up with a better metaphor twenty years later in *The World is Flat*, but we think that the "flat" world he described was not so different from the "smaller" one we foresaw. *The Franchise Advantage* was directed to business owners, prospective franchisees and the general reader. It remains, in our humble opinion, as comprehensive a study of franchising as has been written. Although out of print, it can be downloaded free by anyone interested in the subject from our web site, francorp.com.

In our second book, *How to Buy and Manage a Franchise*, co-authored with Joseph Mancuso and published in 1993, we addressed franchising from the franchisee's perspective. It can also be downloaded at no cost from francorp.com.

What has changed since publication of *The Franchise Advantage?* Many things cultural and economic, some of which we have attempted to address in Chapter 1. One thing not described in detail in Chapter 1 is the increased complexity of franchising itself. That subject is indeed the primary reason for this present volume and is dealt with at length in the remaining chapters.

This book is not for the general reader. It is specifically designed to answer at length a critically important question that ought to be asked by any owner of a successful business who needs additional distribution outlets in order to grow. That question consists of three parts:

- Should I consider franchising?
- Is my business franchiseable?
- If it is, how do I create a franchise program?

If you are such a person and are curious about the answers, we invite you to read on.

Chapter 1

The Rules Have Changed

The author Isaac Asimov has said, "It is change, continuing change, inevitable change that is the dominant factor in society today." Nowhere is that more true than in the business world, and especially true in the past decade. Computers, the Internet, and hand-held communication devices have vastly altered the way we process and store information and, of course, communicate. But changes have occurred in all business sectors. In retailing, the downtown department store as the major focal point for shopping was replaced by the enclosed mall. Later, enclosed mall development slowed as "big box" mega-discount stores gained popularity. Chains that had been flourishing began to founder. They could not compete in an atmosphere of steep discounts sustainable only by extraordinarily high sales levels. By the end of the millennium the restaurant industry, which exploded during the second half of the twentieth century with considerable help from franchising, hit a saturation point. Many of the biggest chains staggered under competitive pressures. In the petroleum industry, major consolidation reduced the number of well-known brands to a few. The airline industry faltered as its leaders faced insolvency driven by rising fuel costs, increased security costs and a discount mania. Ultra large law firms merged into ultra, ultra large law firms. People began moving from the suburbs back to the city (how unusual!). The health care industry underwent major trauma in the crossfire between insurance rates, rising hospital costs, nurse shortages, capitation of insurance coverages and outrageous malpractice awards.

No wonder then that franchising has also changed. For one thing, traditional mom and pop franchise buyers gave way to more sophisticated candidates with better education, more capital and more business experience. These people were the laid-off victims of downsized, merged, bankrupt or obsolescent companies, and they started buying franchises in record numbers. And as franchisees they were ideal! No franchise operators have a better chance of success than people who come from a structured big-company environment. Those who are accustomed to following a system, adapting to procedures, observing dress code, and obeying the employee manual and rules of behavior become ideal candidates for a franchise, where the ability and willingness to follow rules is crucial. But the nature of franchising has changed, too. Franchising was once the domain of small maverick entrepreneurs, such as Ray Kroc of McDonald's, Kemmons Wilson of Holiday Inn and Colonel Sanders of Kentucky Fried Chicken. They have been replaced in the modern era by more sophisticated entrepreneurs whose names are less familiar than their companies. Today's entrepreneurs are often armed with MBAs, meaningful work experience, sufficient capital, and a new alien object called a "business plan." But don't think we still don't have our share of wide-eyed junior Ray Krocs, Kemmons Wilsons or Colonel Sanders. We do. And even this new breed of franchisor is more highly qualified than his or her predecessor. Of course all new franchisors have a wealth of experience to fall back upon: the experience of predecessors who came up with the right way – or in some cases the wrong way – to become a franchisor. The early folks had no role models. A banker in Hong Kong told us in the early 1980's, when we were considering taking some of our US clients into China: "The companies who will succeed in China will be those who step over the bones of the pioneers. Don't be a pioneer." Ray Kroc, Kemmons Wilson and Colonel Sanders were pioneers, but the graveyards are full of the unmarked headstones of pioneers who didn't make it. We often characterize our company, Francorp, Inc., which since 1976 has been the largest developer of franchises in the world, as an observer watching thousands of entrepreneurs parachute into a jungle. We simply wait to see who can make it through the jungle to safety. Out they come, crawling on their hands and knees, heads bandaged, arms in slings, bruised and bleeding, but in the process their businesses have survived and may indeed be ready for exceptional growth.

The lessons learned from what worked and what didn't work in business became the basis for the standards for the franchising industry. The successful companies were those who learned from their own experience or that of someone else. Those who tried to shortcut the process or left out an important part of the recipe failed. That part has not changed. But what has changed is the fact that it is much more difficult to become a franchisor today than it was in the past. Registration and filing requirements are more stringent and lawsuits have proliferated. The economy forgives fewer mistakes and profit margins are lower, making it harder for companies to survive prolonged cyclical changes. Meanwhile, increasing numbers of companies with huge market share and economic clout exert additional pressure on new and growing companies.

At one time having a large business tended to insure survival in any economy. That, too, has changed. Of the top one hundred businesses of fifty years ago, only a handful exist today. The others have been acquired, merged, or are bankrupt. Our good friend, Arthur Lipper, publisher of Venture magazine and Chairman of New York and Foreign Securities Corporation, once said: "The best way to have a small business is to buy a big business and wait." In the past, most of the growth in the economy was from big businesses getting bigger, adding more people and more branches in more cities and more countries and adding new products and services. Today the growth of the business sector stems principally from small and new businesses. It is comical to hear politicians point to layoffs by big companies as indicative of the problems in the economy. Let's not blame the economy when the real culprits are businesses with outmoded business models and inappropriate products and services that fail to adjust to changes in the marketplace. Politicians look for ways to help these big companies survive, when in reality they should be doing more to encourage small business development, because that is where the real growth is taking place.

Of course, one force that has dramatically changed the face of business in general and franchising in particular is technology, with special emphasis on the Internet. Newspapers, magazines and franchise shows, which were the principal sources of prospective franchise leads, have given way big time to the Internet. For the price of one ad in the Wall Street Journal or Entrepreneur magazine, a franchisor can be listed on eight different franchise-sales portals on the Internet. The results have been mind-boggling. We will deal with this whole Internet phenomenon in a later chapter, but it certainly has had a major impact on the growth of franchising and in the way franchise companies operate. The Internet has also given rise to a large number of new Internet-related businesses that are franchising.

The changes that are occurring are not simply reactions to recessions or booms. There are always three cycles that create the highs and lows. The first *expansion* cycle typically lasts from two to five years, during which time the economy gets better and better. This cycle is inevitably followed by *recession*. At that point the balloon bursts into a death spiral, sometimes causing a depression, but at the very least a drop in the economy characterized by unemployment, unfavorable business climates and cutbacks in spending and employment. Eventually, cycle two bottoms out and then we have *recovery*, the link between recession and expansion that usually lasts a few years before the economy starts to heat up again and we go through the process again. *Expansion, recession, recovery... expansion, recession, recovery.* This progression has not changed, but what has changed is that expansion cycles are lasting longer and the recession cycles are less severe – that is unless you happen to be unemployed. And, indeed, the principal casualty of recession has been the large company employee. Pardon us for drooling, but for people in the franchising business this couldn't be better. As we noted earlier, ex-large company employees make ideal franchise candidates. Not only do they come from the right work environment, they are usually financially qualifed, with 401K cash, severance pay and equity in their homes. (Fully 70 per cent of the people who buy a franchise refinance their homes.) Today, these folks buy franchises from small businesses and entrepreneurs who started their businesses, began to grow them, but lacked capital to open more stores or offices. Unable to borrow or persuade people to invest in their companies, they decided to franchise.

2004 saw what we like to call Franchising's Perfect Storm, the confluence of three phenomena that fueled explosive franchise growth in the franchising industry. In the previous few years, more than twenty-one million people age 25-54 had dropped out of the US labor force. Then, in the first six weeks of that year, twenty-two IPOs were issued compared to an average of two each during the same period in the three previous years. In March of 2004 alone, forty-four companies went public. Meanwhile, interest rates for business loans had dropped from 22 per cent in 1980 to 10 per cent in 2004 and mortgage rates from 14 per cent in 1980 to 6 per cent in 2004. So you had a perfect opportunity for franchisors to find franchise buyers who could borrow money inexpensively in a strong economy with a rising stock market. Notwithstanding the political rhetoric in the primary election campaigns between George W. Bush and John Kerry, people felt confident in the economy and many of them – even the unemployed – had available capital. This Perfect Storm environment lasted through the end of 2006.

Buying habits have also changed. Today, millions of people buy products off the Internet. But even that phenomenon has been altered in recent years. More and more Internet companies have developed a "click and brick" presence as they came to recognize that buyers want a place where they can actually see and touch merchandise offered on the Internet and return merchandise purchased there.

The relatively new phenomenon of outsourcing also brought significant changes to the economy. Outsourcing affected businesses positively by enabling companies to buy products and services more cheaply and eliminate higher priced products and employees. And while outsourcing brought consumers lower prices, it caused many employees to lose their jobs. In addition, many old war-horse industries that pulled the economy out of the doldrums in the past were very much weakened or even banished. The steel and automobile industries, although making a comeback after a severe decline, would never own the market again. Defense spending, while still present, was no longer a dominant factor positively affecting the economy. Housing, while still in demand, would never attain postwar baby-boom levels. The whirlpool caused by business downsizing during and after recessions became a death spiral in which budget and personnel cuts were the norm. Only the more efficient businesses and those that were counter-cyclical, such as Wal-Mart, Home Depot and other niche businesses, flourished.

So where do these changes leave you, today's business owner? For one thing you must be more flexible. You don't have the slack in the line to stay with an entrenched strategy if it isn't working. You have to be able to monitor, evaluate, analyze, correct, change and adapt. You must also have a clear view of this changing world from a big picture perspective. You can't operate with a shopkeeper's mentality, thinking that the world consists of the block where you are located and the people who are your customers. You have got to read the major publications, stay in touch with what is going on in the economy, be aware of industry trends and changes. You must constantly reassess the traditional strategies of business expansion and pick and choose those that fit your mode of doing business most effectively. Never let your competition run your business. Just because a competitor is giving away its products at a ridiculously low price does not mean that you should try to match them. Boston Chicken made that mistake. The original Boston Chicken units were strictly carry-out restaurants that made rotisserie chicken and served delicious corn, baked beans, and salads on the side. They operated in small spaces with minimal staff and because they roasted several chickens on a skewer at the same time it was easy to take them off the skewer, chop them in half and throw half on each plate, adding sides. Low food costs, low labor, efficient operations. Along came McDonald's. They opened a competing business called Hearth Express, which offered the same products that Boston Chicken served but added meat loaf, baked ham and seating. Boston Chicken panicked. They, too, added meat loaf, ham and seating and raised $1 billion to finance their growth and that of their franchisees. Within two years after opening Hearth Express, McDonald's realized that the units were not meeting their financial goals and shut the company down. By this time Boston Chicken had hundreds of units operating that were also under-performing financially. At last, Boston Chicken folded. And who bought them out of bankruptcy? Who else? McDonald's!

Chapter 2

The Way To Get Left Behind

For many business owners, the decision to look at franchising as an expansion alternative comes when they find themselves at a crossroads. Their business is successful. It is making money. The question is: how best to make it grow? One man we met recently found himself in just such a situation. He had devised a new business concept that he believed could be expanded nationally. But he lacked the capital to undertake an aggressive growth program. He knew, however, that time waits for no man. "Whenever I pick up a trade journal my heart stops," he told us. "I'm afraid somebody else will do it before I do."

Hundreds, perhaps thousands of CEOs, corporate executives and business owners have similar dilemmas. Whether they have a new concept to introduce, an existing business in need of faster growth, or just more demands on capital than they can satisfy with existing resources, they all face critical decisions. Should they take the plunge and risk losses – even the loss of the business itself – or proceed cautiously and perhaps miss the chance of a lifetime? Actually, most managers in this situation have little choice. They cannot risk betting the company on an exciting new concept. Like our friend, they mutter wistfully, "If only there were a way to get the job done without excessive risk." So what are the options? Should you consider expanding at all? Our feeling is that if you own a business and are reading this book to learn more about franchising, you have already answered that question. You do want to grow your business. Your specific goal may not be the same as someone else's. You may want to expand your company in order to sell it. You may want to eventually pass it on to your children. You may have a dream to take it public. But the question "Should I?" has already been answered. What remains is the question "How?"

The answer to that will depend greatly upon your individual personality, experience and abilities. We frequently conduct seminars on franchising for business owners and executives. But even if all of the people in attendance at our seminars owned the same type of business, no two would be in precisely the same situation. One might have a lot of capital, another very little. One might have extensive experience in running a sizeable company, another limited experience at running a small one. One might have family working in the business. One might have a burning desire to grow this business as fast and as far as possible. Another might be conservative and have a comfort zone only for slow growth. All of these factors contribute to the decision on how to expand.

But for a moment let's consider the consequenes of not expanding. The first consequence is loss of momentum. In business, you don't simply stand still if you're not moving forward; you begin to fall behind and may soon be out of the game.

Why don't companies expand? Three reasons:

1. Lack of capital
2. Lack of dedicated people
3. Lack of vision

Ironically, these are almost the same three reasons companies franchise:

1. Lack of capital
2. Lack of qualified people
3. The need or desire to move more rapidly.

The major impediment to your ability to expand is probably capital. To expand takes money. Whether you are driving an 18-wheeler, an SUV or a passenger car, you need fuel. Money is the fuel you need to drive your expansion. We know of only four ways to get it.

The four ways to raise expansion capital

1. Internally generated capital. This is the money that you make in your business. We hate to be the bearers of bad tidings, but here are a few facts: Fact #1 – You will never make any real money running your business. Fact

#2 – You will never generate enough liquidity out of your current business to open several company-owned units out of cash flow. Fact #3 – The better your business does, the more money you will need to invest or borrow to fuel your expansion.

Hard to believe? Let's take a look. Review your own financial statements from last year. Are your profits reflected in your bank account today? Probably not. Why? Because you continue to put cash back into your business to add inventory, hire people, advertise, and update equipment. In doing so, you do increase the value of your business on the balance sheet, but you do not really increase your liquidity and therefore lack the cash to fund expansion. You would agree, we are sure, that 20 percent earnings on your invested capital would be an excellent return. The companies on the New York Stock Exchange average only about a 7.5 percent return annually. Not on sales; we are talking about return on invested capital, the money it takes to establish a new store, branch, restaurant, office or whatever. Even if you were able consistently to earn 20 percent and keep it in your bank account, it would be five years before you would have enough cash to open the next unit without debt or outside financing.

So the sad truth is, you will never make any real money running your business on a day-to-day basis, even with a handsome 20 percent return on investment. You can make a good living, but you will never make any real money.

Internally generated capital is simply not sufficient to fuel any kind of aggressive expansion.

2. Borrowed Capital. Of course, you can try to borrow the money. But borrowing has two major disadvantages. First, you can only borrow up to your net worth or possibly 1½ times your net worth, depending upon current banking standards. But the net worth/collateral of most companies and individuals is simply too small to allow expansion at a level aggressive enough to capitalize on market opportunities. Second, borrowed money must usually be paid back. Banks are funny that way. And payback can be really tough when you are putting money into a new business that will probably lose money in the first year and barely break even in the second.

Most bank loans are five-year loans, requiring that you pay 20 percent of the principal each year for five years in addition to interest. The interest can run from as low as 8 percent to as high as 22 percent, which we saw in the 1980's. On that basis, you must repay an amount equal to 30 percent (20 percent on the principle plus 10 percent interest) of the loan in each of those first two years when you are not making any money! Where will that money come from? From your present business, of course. Now if you should be so fortunate (or unfortunate) as to have sufficient collateral to open two or three new units, you then find yourself having to pay a whopping 58 percent of those loans for the first two years. This could be disastrous. Opening multiple units, whether with borrowed capital, cash flow, or a combination of both is sort of like having quintuplets. They all wake up at the same time, cry at the same time, have to be fed at the same time, changed at the same time, and go through the same baby steps at the same time. It is a lot easier when you space your children two years apart, so that by the time you have the third one the four-year old can run and answer the phone for you while you are changing the baby.

Borrowing money to open additional units is the worst answer to a difficult problem. First, it does not allow you to employ a sufficiently aggressive roll-out strategy. Second, borrowing to open any new units places enormous stress on your existing business. You must service these loans at a time when you are least capable of doing so, while increasing the burden of retaining employees, training them, and expecting them to perform at maximum levels.

Bankers, it seems, are always there when you don't need them. When interest rates are high and unaffordable to small business owners, the banks are quick to offer money at those exorbitant rates. After all, banks recognize that small or rapidly expanding businesses have a higher risk, but they reason that high rates make it worth that risk. But when interest rates are very low and enticing to business owners, banks don't want you. Banks would rather lend $1 million to one large company than $200,000 each to five small or medium size businesses. There is only one account to service, and the minimal odds of the large company defaulting on a loan reduce the risk.

3. Equity capital. For most business owners, the odds of getting someone to invest in their company for expansion, particularly for opening additional company-owned units, are slim to none; and Slim just went home. Why? Because as was stated earlier, there is no real money to be made in operating company-owned units – at least not the kind of money investors and venture capitalists are looking for. They are looking for a return of 50-70 percent annually on their investment, which is possible only by getting it in waysother than by operating units. Your dream of finding investors who will give you the money to open ten more stores is simply not realistic. Investors may invest in your business, but only because within three to four years they expect you to implement an exit strategy with three options:

a. You sell the company and they cash out.
b. You buy them out and they cash out.
c. You take the company public and they cash out.

Venture capitalists are not interested in getting into a ten-year investment program, even though your business plan may forecast great returns by that point. They need to turn their investments over in a relatively short period of time, usually within three to four years. Think about it. If you buy a common stock, do you buy it because you want the 23 cents per share quarterly dividend? No, of course not. You buy it at $2 because you expect it to go to $3, then $10 and then $20 in a few years. In other words, you expect to make money not on the company's earnings but on the appreciation of the company's value or of the market in general. Many of the stocks people buy and sell are in companies that never made money before they bought it and still had not made money when they sold it at a far higher price than they paid for it. A rising tide lifts all boats. When the market is up, all stocks go up. When the President has the sniffles, stocks go down. And, at the risk of redundancy, we repeat, real money is not made by operating units.

Sophisticated investors want to invest in businesses with strong management capable of building a company to many times its present size. If you are the vice president of marketing for a major food chain and you want to expand, start a new food concept, or acquire a new company, you can probably find investors to back you. But as a successful operator of a small restaurant chain seeking capital to open additional restaurants, your chances are far less favorable. That is the case even if you have a well-articulated business plan that clearly defines the concept, the company, the market, the competition, the opportunity, the alternatives for expansion, and your growth strategy. It is the case even if your plan includes a five-year cash flow analysis that provides good evidence that an investment in your firm would be appropriate. But supposing you have such a business plan and do, against all odds, attract an investor. What that investor will demand as he turns over his money is the right to step in and take control of your company. No matter what percentage of ownership he acquires, if you do not attain the goals stated in your Business Plan or if, after you have achieved your goals, he feels you are not capable of managing the monster that you have created, he can exercise power over you. The conflict between owners and investors is endemic in the relationship. Owners want to build the company and investors want to cash out. Owners may also find it difficult to have to answer to the investor or even to give him a voice in the way the company is operated.

4. Franchising. Did we say franchising? Weren't we were talking about ways of raising money for expansion? Well, as a matter of fact, we are, and franchising may be the best-kept secret for acquiring expansion capital in the world of business. Think about it. Someone pays you a franchise fee – usually at least $35,000 – for the right to use your name, your system of operation, and to have you teach them the business and to help them get started. They also pay you a royalty – a percentage of their sales on an ongoing basis (usually about 6 percent) – for the right to use your name and your system and for your continued consulting and assistance in their ongoing operation. In other words, as a franchisor you are never dependent upon a single bank or a single investor. Every franchisee becomes both an investor and a vital, cooperative part of the growth of your business.

But franchising offers other advantages as well. It solves the unit management problem because franchises are almost always sold to owner/operators who become the managers of their businesses. You, the franchisor, get a much more highly motivated day-to-day manager than you could possibly hire, someone who has a huge (remember, 70 percent take out home equity loans) investment in the business and is totally committed to its success.

Franchising also allows you to grow at a much more rapid rate than would be possible with your own capital. We'll discuss these and other benefits later, but for now, let's focus on how franchising enables you to get the capital you need to expand your business so you don't get left behind. Do the math. Many companies sell more than ten franchises their first year. Ten buyers at $35,000 each gives you $350,000, without loan payments, and without giving up equity in your company. Each franchisee comes to your place of business at no salary and gets on-the-job training – usually for a few months. Then the franchisee goes out and buys the land and builds the building or rents the space, buys the equipment, buys the inventory, buys the fixtures, provides the working capital, and pays to advertise the grand opening – all without any contingent liability on your part.

Your responsibility is to be selective in choosing franchisees. You will train them intensively, assist them in finding a suitable site or defining their territory, and help them get started. Finally, you will be supportive as a consultant and will mentor them once they are in the operation. To put it simply, franchising may be the best way to raise the capital you need to expand your company. To go out and try to borrow money or attempt to bring in investors in today's market, you would have to be a masochist and love pain.

**

But the bigger issue is that the world is not going to sit around and wait until you get ready to open ten or 100 or 1,000 clones of your business. So, if you don't have an unlimited bank account, you've got to find another way to expand – or be left behind.

Chapter **3**

What Franchising Is And What It's Not

It is one thing to know that franchising provides an alternative to internally generated capital, borrowed money or equity funding and quite another to know whether franchising is the right growth system for any specific business or any specific business owner. To answer that, it's helpful to begin by learning precisely what franchising is and what it is not.

The Federal Trade Commission defines franchising as follows:

Franchising is a method of doing business by which the franchisee is granted the right to engage in the business of offering, selling or distributing goods or services under a marketing plan or system prescribed in substantial part by a franchisor and which is substantially associated with the franchisor's trademark, name, logo or advertising.

That's quite a mouthful. To summarize, a franchise exists when the following three elements are in place:

1. You permit someone to use your name.
2. You permit someone to use your system of operation or marketing program.
3. You receive payment of a fee, either initially or on an on-going basis.

If only two of these three elements are present, your business is not a franchise. In fact, some businesses avoid the compliance requirements that are attached to franchising by eliminating either use of the name or use of the system. They sell licenses instead of franchises. (Every franchise involves a license, but not every licensor is a franchisor.) For example, Coca Cola can license someone to imprint the name Coca Cola on T-shirts and sell them. The licensee pays an initial fee and a price for each shirt sold. The licensee has not bought a franchise. When it does sell a franchise (and they are expensive!), the Coca Cola company gives the franchisee the use of its name, its private syrup, the right to bottle and distribute its products in an exclusive territory, a marketing strategy, assistance in developing the market and other benefits – in short a package that includes all three elements listed above. Among other things licensed are technologies, such as software programs, and recipes for special food products that will be used in the licensee's business, providing that the business does not bear the licensor's name. If you are a famous chef such as Wolfgang Puck, for example, and have developed a special Wolfgang Barbeque Sauce, you can offer an exclusive license to restaurants that might want to put a tag line "featuring Wolfgang Barbeque Sauce" beneath the restaurant name. The restaurants will use their own names, not Wolfgang Puck's, and will pay a license fee in addition to a price for the product.

The principal disadvantage of licensing compared with franchising is that the licensor has minimal control over the people to whom he or she grants the license. And the fact that licensors are relatively unregulated compared to franchisors does not compensate for the lack of control. However, the bigger issue is not how to devise a way to avoid being considered a franchise and therefore avoid complying with franchise laws, but rather what is the best business decision for the expansion of your business. If it is important for you to (1) create brand awareness by having people use your name and your system of operation, (2) ensure quality control, and (3) obtain ongoing income from the continued use of your name and system, then franchising is probably the way to go.

How franchising works

As we mentioned earlier, the concept of franchising is simple. Someone pays you an initial franchise fee for the right to use your name and system of operation, and to have you teach them how to operate the business and provide ongoing consulting and assistance. That person then works for you for a month or two learning the business at his or her own expense and pays all the costs of establishing a replica of your business. That includes buying the land, building the building, buying the equipment, making the leasehold improvements, buying the inventory, furnishings, fixtures and signage, and providing all of the working capital needed to establish this business and operate it on an ongoing basis. The franchisee may, in addition, buy equipment and supplies from you, the franchisor. The franchisee will pay a continuing royalty as well. The term "royalty" refers mostly to the license concept of paying a fee for the continued use of the name or system. Royalties are usually paid weekly as a percentage of gross sales. The franchisee is allowed to use your trademark and system and you, in turn, will provide on-going consulting and support.

There are two broad categories of franchises: start-up and conversion. The vast majority of franchises are start-up, a new version of the franchisor's existing business at a new location. Most are sold to individuals who know nothing about the business. A few know nothing about any business. On the first day of training, the fast-food franchisor holds a chicken by the legs and says, "This is a chicken. It has two legs and usually weighs about 2 ½ pounds. We cut this chicken up into eight or nine pieces." etc., etc. Because many franchisees have little or no business experience, it is extremely important that the franchisee become completely familiar with the franchisor's business before opening the doors of his or her own establishment. It is also important to provide comprehensive Operations Manuals so that everything taught during training can be reviewed later. It is also invaluable for use by the franchisee in teaching employees.

Conversion franchises are sold to an individual or group already in the same business, operating under their own name. The most widely known application of conversion franchises has been in the real estate and hardware industries. A real estate owner would take down the sign that said Don's Real Estate and replace it with a new sign that said Century 21—Don's Real Estate. The name Century 21 would occupy 80 percent of the space on the sign and the name of the previous business 20 percent. Ace Hardware is another example. Independent hardware store owners replaced their signs with the Ace Hardware signs. They, too, often identified themselves by adding their own names so that people did not think they went out of business.

In recent years conversion franchising has been employed more and more often by manufacturers. Companies such as United Carbide (marble care), Novus Windshield Repair, Dahlberg, Inc. (hearing aids), and Four Seasons Marketing (solariums) have replaced independent distributors with franchises. The advantage to the manufacturers is higher quality, more dedicated distributors who market their products exclusively. The advantage to franchisees is improved service, including stronger advertising programs.

Most people who buy start-up franchises want to get into an established business that is operating successfully and be taught to operate that business by those who have made it successful. The driving force behind conversion franchises is usually advertising, business systems and purchasing power.

In addition to deriving income from initial franchise fees, royalties and, sometimes, the sale of products or services, the franchisor also collects advertising fees from franchisees. These fees are kept in a separate fund and spent only on advertising aimed at generating customers for all franchisee-and company-owned outlets. They should not be used for any other purpose. Strict records must be kept of all expenses associated with creating or administering the franchise co-op advertising program. Typically, franchisors provide quarterly and annual reports showing the state of the advertising fund.

In both the start up and conversion categories, there are three types of franchises:

Individual Franchise. Most franchises are sold to one individual for one physical location or one territory. A restaurant, muffler shop, beauty salon, or hotel, of course, operates in a fixed location. But for some businesses, such as temporary office placement, carpet cleaning, industrial products sales, or accounting services, the precise location is irrelevant, even though the franchises are assigned a specific territory. Businesses with fixed locations must select sites where demographics will support the business. For example, even though Sun City, Arizona has a population of 40,000, you would not put a USA Baby's Room store in that market. Notwithstanding Viagra, there probably hasn't been a birth there in thirty years! Some businesses base their customer demographics on population density, i.e. one store for every 25,000 people. Other businesses base their customer demographics on the number of cars that drive by the location each day. Population density might be a good criterion for a physical fitness establishment. Drive-by density might work better for a quick lube or fast food operation.

Multiple Unit Franchises (also called master or territorial franchises): The multi-unit franchisee, unlike the individual franchisee, is given a specific territory in which they are required to open a specific number of units on a scheduled basis. Typically you discount the initial franchise fee and require the multi-unit franchisee to pay half of the aggregate amount due for all of the franchises at the execution of the contract. As each unit is opened, they pay the balance of the franchise fee due on that unit. For example, if the individual franchise fee were $35,000, you might discount it to $30,000 for a multiple buyer. Thus, if the multiple buyer buys a ten-unit territory for $300,000, you would collect $150,000 when the contract is executed and $15,000 as each unit is opened. The franchisee might be required to open one unit in the first year, two units in the second year, three in the third year and four in the fourth year. If at any time they did not open a unit on schedule, they would forfeit the money paid in advance but could continue to operate units already opened, so long as those units remained in conformance with operating standards.

Subfranchising: Some franchisors over the years have sold large territories to sales oriented individuals or groups who, in turn, sell individual franchises in their market and service them. Subfranchising, as this method is called, has been used primarily by conversion franchises or franchises with low volume businesses. In the past, Century 21, for example, would sell a large geographical territory – sometimes a whole state – to an individual who set out to persuade independent real estate brokers within that territory to become Century

21 franchisees. The people who bought the rights to these markets had two basic functions. First, they sold the franchises and split the franchise fees with the franchisor. Second, they provided ongoing consulting services to these offices and split the royalties with the franchisor. They usually did not operate a real estate office themselves.

The goals of franchising

Whatever franchise strategy is chosen, the goal of the franchisor is to create value for everyone involved. The franchisor must create a network of franchises that produces enough revenue to return a profit on the licensing of its name, technology, system and ongoing assistance. The franchisees must also benefit through profits and through the achievement of the American Dream of business ownership. Though franchisees use the franchisor's name and business system they are nonetheless independent owners. Ultimately, consumers must also benefit by gaining access to a well-managed business that provides desirable, fairly-priced goods or services.

One of the bywords of franchising is "consistency." The very term "franchising" has come to be regarded as synonymous with consistency. Franchises are almost always used by middle of the road businesses that seek to attract the broadest possible market. Holiday Inns are not usually the very best hotels in every town, although in some towns they may be. They are not aimed at the high profile market sought by the Four Seasons or the Ritz Carltons of the world. McDonald's is not a "fine dining, white tablecloth" restaurant. Great Clips is probably not where the stars go to have their hair done before they appear on a late night television show. But all of these businesses have one thing in common, consistency. If you drive into a strange town with your family looking for a place to eat, you are less likely to pull in at Don's Diner than McDonald's. If you saw Don's Motel or a Comfort Inn, you would probably go to the Comfort Inn. If you needed a haircut, and you saw Don's Barbershop or Great Clips, you would go to Great Clips. Need we say more? So don't believe the myths that franchising is fast food only, that consistency is to be scoffed at, that only small businesses franchise, or that franchises quality is sacrificed. We have heard all of the disparaging comments. All one needs to do is to look at how franchising has grown in the United States and around the world in the past half century. Franchising continues to be utilized as a growth system by a wide variety of businesses, including healthcare, high tech, the automotive aftermarket, Internet-related businesses, home furnishings industry, medical, legal, banking, and myriad others. Even big businesses make use of franchising. Krystal Hamburgers had 400 units in operation when it decided to franchise. Mrs. Fields Cookies had hundreds of units in operation when it started franchising. Hyatt Hotels was already a large chain when it started franchising.

Of course, franchising has always been the perfect vehicle for the undercapitalized small entrepreneur with a good idea. Kemmons Wilson of Holiday Inn, Ray Kroc of McDonald's, and Colonel Sanders of Kentucky Fried Chicken were franchising pioneers. All were small entrepreneurs who grew wealthy by sharing their ideas with ambitious people eager for a piece of the American Dream.

Far from sacrificing quality, franchising usually raises it. Our experience before becoming franchise consultants was in managing companies that both operated company-owned units and sold franchises. In nearly every instance when our companies sold off a company-owned unit to a franchisee, sales went up. In almost every instance in which we bought out a franchisee and put in our own manager, sales went down. There is simply no substitute for the owner-operator with a vested interest in his or her business. They are highly motivated people who stick it out because their financial lives depend on it.

Who qualifies

But let's face it, franchising is not for everyone. As a business owner, if you like to keep total control over your business, or if you believe that no one in the world is going to operate that business as well as you do, then you should probably not franchise. You should probably not even expand to any extent, even with company-owned units. You are probably better off staying as you are. Or, if you expect franchising to be an easy, quick way to untold riches, you may also be disappointed. Some people we talk to say they want to be as big as McDonald's or bigger. Yet, after a little probing, it's apparent that they have little understanding of the financial, operational, infrastructure, marketing, and overall expansion realities. Let's face it. Some of us are just not destined to be Number 1 in our class. That doesn't mean that with more realistic expectations we can't be extremely successful. At our Francorp offices in Chicago, we get thousands of calls from people who want to franchise their businesses. But when some who come in for a meeting talk about getting rich quick and having thousands of units, we press a secret button opening a trap door that drops them twenty floors to their death in the alligator pit. Although we have exaggerated a bit and don't really have an alligator pit or a trap door, sometimes we wish we did. The truth is, just as in your business, there is no secret get rich quick scheme. In franchising, as in every other endeavor, hard work and talent propel you ahead. "Techies" who lack marketing or people skills or others who are good at giving orders but not good at teaching, are not going to succeed in franchising. "Superstars" and "loners" don't work well in franchising. Your success in franchising will be related more to how good a coach you are than how good a player you are.

In summary, franchising can offer a wonderful opportunity to the right person with the right business. Let's explore in greater detail how a successful franchise is created.

Chapter 4

Creating A Franchiseable Business

Whether or not you own a business or simply have an idea for a business, it is important before making a decision to use franchising as a growth system to know what qualities that business needs to be successful in franchising...and what qualities it does not need. In assessing the franchiseability of any business, three broad areas are critical:

1. The business concept and structure
2. The marketability of the business
3. The abilities and commitment of the owner/franchisor

Let's take them one at a time.

The business concept and structure

What is the single most overrated requirement for franchising? Answer: A Great New Concept. Sound crazy? Think about it. Some of the most successful franchise companies are McDonald's, Subway, Holiday Inn, Midas Muffler, Service Master, Great Clips, and Jani King. But all of these businesses had many predecessors. None of their concepts was unique. Next question: What is the second most overrated requirement for franchising? Answer: A Great Quality Product. Consider the giant hamburger franchises. In voting for the highest quality hamburger, McDonald's has consistently been picked third behind Burger King and Wendy's in consumer surveys. Yet in an industry in which these three companies have a combined 72 percent market share, Wendy's, which surveys say has the best burger, owns only a 12 percent share. Burger King, which came in second has a 19 percent share, and McDonald's, picked last of the Big 3 has a whopping 41 percent share. So, before you bet the farm, mortgage the house, quit your job and withdraw all of your savings to start franchising your existing business because you believe you have a great concept or a fabulous product, consider what those companies that have succeeded in franchising do have. If the concept isn't always great and the product isn't always fabulous, what's their secret? Answer: their operating systems. Of the three, McDonald's not only has the biggest market share, it has the best operating system. That's why 97 percent of all Americans go into a McDonald's every year and 59 percent every month.

McDonald's is the poster child for franchising simply because McDonald's outperforms everyone else. Location, layout, consistency, product quality (one virtue among many), speed of service, advertising, focus on the kid market, Beanie Babies, McFlurries, NFL and Disney promotions, and the fastest drive-thru in the business are all characteristics of McDonald's. In units with drive-thru windows, up to 85 percent of sales are made at those windows. In many markets, McDonald's has increased unit efficiency, lowered costs and overcome the shortage of help by outsourcing the voice on the squawk box to India. That's right. When you pull up to the speaker in the drive-thru, the voice that welcomes you to McDonald's and asks for your order may well be that of someone in Bangalore. With this one innovation, McDonald's has cut thirty seconds off the drive-thru time and increased sales system-wide by millions of dollars. It's not about the burgers, the mufflers, the whatevers. It's about systems of operation that work smoothly and are duplicable. Those who thrive – or even survive – are the ones that put it all together: the concept, a strong pilot unit, marketing, advertising, operations, pricing, consistency, profitability, locations, and, in franchising, selection, training and support of their franchise owners. The marketplace is a vast field full of land mines for businesses. Trigger one, and it could be fatal. Make a mistake on products, location, advertising, pricing, size of your market, the competition, and it could all be over.

Of course, if you do have a great concept, like Curves, or a fabulous product, like Starbucks (not a franchise), it can't hurt. In fact, it can help make you wealthy and famous. But even then, a great concept is the frosting on the cake. First, to be successful in franchising, you need the cake.

The Prototype

To franchise you must have a profitable operating prototype. The prototype may be your principal business or it may be a version of it designed for franchising. You may decide, for example, that your business will be easier to operate and more profitable if you eliminate some of the marginal products or services you offer now, maybe even reduce its size and place it in a different location. How long should you be in business before you franchise? Of course, the longer you've been established, the greater your credibility. But, like concept and product, age is not a critical factor. If you have no business and are still in the concept stage, you can follow the suggestions given here to build a business worthy of being franchised. But whatever stage you are in, you will not be ready to sell franchises until your prototype is up and operating and until it is generating positive cash flow. Until you have proved that the business works and can make money, you are not ready for prime time. The last thing you want to do is sell tickets for the Titanic!

The prototype needs to be lean and mean, which means that before franchising you must examine it for weak spots. Like a pinhole in a balloon that becomes larger as the balloon inflates, expansion will expose the weaknesses in your operation. If you wait until you start franchising to fix those problems, the likelihood is that the franchisee will not be able to patch all the holes as well as you can—if you can sell franchises at all. If your company has multiple units now, you have a different challenge. You may have central purchasing, central payroll and even centralized hiring. When you franchise, your franchisees will have to do things your current managers do not do now. One of the first tasks Francorp does when we take on a new client is to identify operational areas that need to be corrected, changed or adjusted for franchising. We often recommend POS (point of sale) systems, equipment, procedures, and policies that make a business more franchiseable.

We mentioned earlier the McDonald's system. Every franchise company actually has two operating systems. One is the franchise system, encompassing all of the elements necessary for creating and operating a franchise. We will address that type of system in later chapters. The second, of course, is the unit operating system. And the McDonald's unit operating system is one that every business would do well to emulate, whether or not it franchises. That system begins with effective procedures for establishing the business and operating on a day-to-day basis. It means selecting the right location or market, having an effective marketing and sales strategy, employing capable people and training them adequately. It includes quality control, good products, the right environment and atmosphere, buying processes, pricing, maintenance, capital ... and on and on. But more than that, it means achieving consistency in all of these activities. A system that works one way this week and another way next week is not a system. It's a recipe for disaster. If you are a business owner who likes to make it up as you go along, even though your business is successful (perhaps because of your own hard work and personality) it is probably not ready for franchising.

Financial controls

Good financial controls are essential to any operating system. Small companies that do their own bookkeeping or accounting should incorporate accounting categories that allow both you and your franchisees to monitor accounting and performance data on a "real time" basis. Hardware and software for this purpose is available and affordable. It can even be tied into video cameras, located in key areas of each unit, that enable both you and the franchisee to observe operations from a remote location. Through these systems, you can obtain up-to-the-moment register readings, number of employees on duty, product mix, customer accounts, payroll, crew hours and other relevant information important to the operation and management of the business.

Large companies will have a different problem. Although good financial controls are likely to be in place, for franchising purposes some direct financial and operational functions heretofore executed at the corporate level may need to be transferred to the unit level. Payroll, accounts payable, accounts receivable, purchasing, depreciation, corporate G&A (general and administrative charges to the individual operating units), and differences in COG (cost of goods) might all be candidates for transfer. For example, if the parent company has been charging an individual store its actual costs of goods purchased or manufactured, but will now take a markup over these costs when it sells them to its franchisees, the accounting system will need to be adjusted accordingly.

Whether your company is large or small, if you eventually have units located in remote areas your financial and operational reporting systems will be of critical importance—not only to your franchise program, but to your existing business. Time and time again clients have told us that some of the best things they got out of franchising were the financial and operational changes we helped them make and the operations manuals we drafted while putting their franchise program together, which strengthened their business in so many ways.

Profitability

And speaking of financial matters, we said that the prototype should have positive cash flow. In other words, be profitable. How profitable? In our opinion, no business should be franchised unless the franchise owner, after the second year of operation, can make the same salary he or she would pay a hired manager of that business, plus a 15 percent return of the franchisee's invested capital. Not 15 percent of sales, but a 15 percent return of invested capital. For example, if a franchisee would need $200,000 to open one of your units, and if the manager's salary for that unit if non-franchised would be $50,000, the franchisee should earn by the end of the second year of operation $80,000 before taxes and debt service. That's $50,000 in salary, plus $30,000, which is 15 percent of their $200,000 investment. We assume it takes two years to get a unit to a mature level.

By the way, when we speak of "profitability," we're referring to the operating unit that will be franchised, not to the corporation that owns it. Your company may be operating at a loss for a variety of reasons that have no bearing on the operating unit. You may have excess staff while you are developing the business, or doing research and development on new products that may or may not be in the franchisee's unit. You may be paying higher than required salaries to family members or to people that you are grooming for higher levels of responsibility. You may also be paying higher rent than your franchisees will pay. These adjustments need to be taken into account, in order to determine if you have a credible model to franchise.

The marketability of the business

We said earlier that age is not a vital factor in franchising. Neither is size. It is wonderful to have been in business for years, have a large number of units in operation, and have brand identity and a growing reputation. But most businesses that start selling franchises have only one operating unit. That fact can actually be attractive to potential franchisees, because it suggests that your business may be in an emerging new industry or that it may cater to an unserved or underserved market niche. Big companies highlight their corporate resources, their training center, their field support, and other corporate strengths. If yours is a one-unit operation and has not been in business very long, you will stress your hands-on assistance and your personal accessibility – the fact that the franchisee will be working directly with the founder, who has a vested interest in their success. Bigness may actually have some disadvantages, which may be one reason that 70 percent of all companies selling franchises have fifty or fewer units. Some of the behemoths of franchising, especially in fast food, are finding it harder and harder to find locations for new units. The same is true of Starbucks, which has all company-owned units. Yet the success of Starbucks has benefited a number of single-unit coffee shop owners who have franchised into a market that didn't exist until Starbucks came along.

If concept and product are not critical, it is nonetheless helpful when thinking about franchising to be able to demonstrate a point of difference between your business and that of your competitors. You may have a unique store design, a special marketing program, a particularly effective way of displaying or delivering your products or services. Sometimes only one element needs to be different to ensure success. For example, price. You may have found a way to offer the same products as other stores but at significantly lower prices. On the other hand, be careful lest the competition adjusts and your advantage evaporates. For example, Checkers, a strictly drive-up, walk-in hamburger-only concept with a 99-cent burger took a run at McDonald's in the 1980s. Within a short time, McDonald's, whose burgers were in the $2.00 range, came out with a 99-cent burger and blew Checkers away.

If you are still at the concept stage and haven't yet established a prototype, be sure that there is a market for your exciting, new, or different product or service. This is especially true if you need to educate the consumer about what you offer. Educating the market is expensive. It takes a great deal of capital to introduce a new concept. Ask yourself if there is a real need for this product or service, which if properly explained to people would sell, or whether you simply believe it to be a great idea. Larger companies do test marketing and focus groups. McDonald's, in selected locations, tested pizza and cheddar cheeseburgers on a whole-wheat bun. Both disappeared after tests did not confirm or justify their continuance. It's always best to back up even a good idea with research. Margot Chapman, one of the top marketing and concept development consultants in the United States, regularly conducts focus groups and market tests for companies like DuPont, NurtaSweet and Allstate. She may be an expert, but that didn't deter her from spending a year researching the market before opening her own Swirlz chain of cup-cake stores.

If you intend to roll out your franchise program nationally or internationally, you should know what you're getting into. Business people in other countries often look at the United States and see a single market. We know better, but US companies often make the same mistake when looking at other countries. For example, Tokyo and Osaka, though only 300 miles apart, are very different. Tokyo is a sophisticated, cosmopolitan city, Osaka more industrialized. Mexico City and Cancun are vastly different. Be sure that the products or services your business sells will be welcomed in whatever markets you intend to enter. Barbeque in Chicago means baby back pork ribs in a red sauce. In Texas, it means beef ribs. In South Carolina, ribs come with a mustard sauce. If your business is water-proofing basements in Chicago, good luck in Florida. They have no basements! Dig two feet and you have water! When Popeyes chicken ventured out of Louisiana, where hot and spicy is a normal and expected component in foods, into Northwest and Midwest markets, unit sales lagged. In time, they learned that they needed a milder version. Do your homework in new markets and see what products and services are being sold successfully by competitors. In the process, you may also learn about opportunities not being addressed in those markets that you can capitalize on. But above all, don't use a franchisee as your guinea pig to see whether or not your concept is adaptable.

Facilities and personnel

One of the keys to successful franchising is your ability to assist franchisees in finding locations for their franchises. In fact, some franchisors do not sell franchises unless the physical location has been identified beforehand, as in a shopping mall. If you have a fast-food concept that requires a food court location, space in existing malls may be extremely hard to find. Typically, mall owners offer available locations to operators with whom they have had experience in other locations and whose operations are high-volume performers, exceeding base rents and thus paying the mall a percentage of total sales. Affordability can also be a factor. A 2,000 square foot location may cost four times as much in New York City as in suburban Denver. For location-sensitive businesses, land costs, liquor licenses, construction costs, availability of suppliers, building codes, personal services licenses, legal requirements, political factors, and other issues need to be explored before entering a market. In some areas, for example, a cosmetologist does not need a license to do procedures such as nails, skin care, or massage. In others, separate licenses are required for each. You also need to be reasonably sure that franchisees will find the personnel they need to operate the business. In markets you intend to enter, what does the job market look like? Are there available cosmetologists to staff your hair salon? Are there experienced chefs for your Hibachi Flat Grill restaurant? Are teenagers available to work in your fast food downtown locations? Will you have to pay higher wages than in your current markets? What affect will this have on unit economics? At worst, it could mean that your business, as you currently operate it, may not be adaptable in certain markets. When they first start to expand, some companies deliberately avoid large urban locations in favor of low-cost land and labor in less-competitive rural and suburban markets. Wal-Mart is the perfect example.

Teachability

To be franchiseable, your business must be marketable not only to consumers but to franchisees. And one of the most critical qualifications for readiness to franchise is teachability. You must be able to teach a franchise owner of normal intelligence how to run the business within four to eight weeks. Some franchises require longer training periods. A McDonald's fran-chisee works two years in a restaurant, often on evenings and weekends, plus three weeks at Hamburger Univer-sity. Domino's Pizza sells franchises only to people who have been managers for two years. Culver's, an outstanding fast food operation featuring frozen custard and their famous Butter Burgers, requires four months of training. Training is absolutely critical. A person might learn to lubricate a car in two days, but it takes much longer to teach that person how to find a site, obtain permits, oversee construction, hire and train staff, do marketing and then run an auto lube business on a day-to-day basis. In franchising, there is a direct correlation between success of franchises and quality, intensity, and duration of training.

Credibility

Another aid to marketability is reputation. Prospective franchisees are human. They respond to success stories. Any favorable publicity, letters or even customer comments about your business will enhance the marketability of your franchise. News stories about your personal accomplishments – whether in business endeavors or contributions to your community – will add to your credibility and make worthwhile additions to your franchise sales brochure. Video clips from TV broadcasts and articles from trade publications or national magazines and newspapers are worth their weight in gold. And if you don't have such publicity – or enough of it – there are ways to get it. You may be surprised to know that much of what you read and see in the media has been generated by public relations people. That's why you hire them. They do write-ups and submit them to the media. You can even do it yourself. Just write a headline accompanied by a story about your business and send it to every media source you can identify in your market. Give it a try. It works. And the reason it works is that print and broadcast media have space and time to fill. Supporting new businesses that may become advertisers can be an excellent way to fill it.

Another way to promote your business is to regularly scan major newspapers and magazines and clip articles and quotes that validate your concept or industry. For example, The Wall Street Journal may report that "widgets are the fastest growing new product in the U.S. this year" or that "pet daycare centers are the newest and most popular trends in the pet industry." If you're in one of those businesses, make sure you retain the articles. If you own a salad restaurant and see an interview on your local TV station that validates your business ("Studies show that vegetarian diets are healthier and contribute to weight loss," for example), call the station and ask for a copy of the interview. Bottom line: media endorsement, whether reported or manufactured, is important and obtainable.

Cost

One would think it goes without saying that the more expensive the business the smaller the pool of prospective franchisees. And yet, that statement is not necessarily true. More important is the amount of up-front cash required of the franchisee investor. And more important yet is the ratio of that investment to the total cost of the business. For example, a franchise that requires the franchisee to pay up-front the total cost of a $100,000 business will be, other things being equal, far less attractive than the franchise that requires a franchisee to pay $100,000 down on a business worth $1,000,000.

Consider the two situations. Franchisee A pays $100,000 down and gets a business worth that amount. But the salary will be low until the buyer can raise sales and profits and therefore increase the value of the business. Yet even if the value doubles, it's still worth only $200,000. Franchisee B, meanwhile, pays the same amount down but must take on debt service. However, the cash flow from a business worth $1,000,000 will both pay the franchisee a higher salary and pay off the debt service. By the time the debt is paid, the franchisee owns a business worth $1,000,000 – and probably a lot more. Who would you rather be?

So one key to marketability is leverage. The higher the percentage of your business that can be financed, the easier it is to sell franchises. Land and buildings, of course, can be financed. So can products and equipment purchased from suppliers. Custom-built equipment and proprietary products are not financeable, nor are leasehold improvements, although often landlords will factor payments on leasehold improvements into the lease. Your goal, then, is to minimize up-front cash required and maximize leverage. Be careful, however, not to allow your franchisees to become over-leveraged with debt service payments that strain their ability to operate comfortably. Understand that before you even begin to offer the first franchise for sale, you should line up financing sources for your franchises. We formed Francorp Capital just for that purpose: to provide financing for our clients' franchises for everything from vehicles to equipment, inventory, computers, working capital, and even for customers of the franchisees who may be purchasing large or costly products. We even arrange credit card processing, which is critical for a new franchise to obtain easily. All these elements make your franchise more saleable and more successful.

The ability and commitment of the owner/franchisor

Do you consider yourself a good manager? Of course you do. But why? Is it because you have built your business single-handedly from the ground up? Is it because no one in the business has worked as many hours as you have? Is it because people genuinely like you and want to be your customers? These are all laudable qualities; but the very traits that have made you successful as an entrepreneur can work against you as a franchisor. We've said it before and we'll say it again:Your success in franchising will depend more upon your teaching and coaching skills than on your ability to carry the company on your shoulders, no matter how broad they are.

Franchising will also test your organizational skills, including your ability to create and manage a complex infrastructure. It may even test them a lot sooner than you expect. For the unprepared, a franchise can very quickly become a monster that's hard to manage. We've seen it happen with our own eyes. Our client, Discovery Zone, sold 160 franchises in the first six months. Another client, Hurricane Wings, sold 65 franchises in the first month. You can readily imagine the impact on these companies. Initial training, site acquisition, construction, startup assistance, grand opening assistance, ongoing field consulting support, coordination of equipment and supplies, printing materials, financing arrangements. All this with companies that had only one unit in operation! Thankfully, there is help available.

This book will help you to understand the elements of franchising. But more important is the meeting you need to have with yourself in a phone booth to decide what it is you really want to do and whether or not you have the ability, desire, and commitment to strap yourself into the pilot's seat of a rocket ship. You will need to shift your style of management from the "hub and spokes" model where all elements report directly to you, to a more structured paradigm, with the eventual establishment of franchise sales, marketing, training, real estate, finance, operations, and legal departments. By no means should you establish and staff any of these departments, initially. You should sell, train and open the first ten units yourself. You need to learn the franchising business before you start adding people. When you – or someone with franchise experience – develop your franchise Business Plan, it will identify the departments you will need, indicate when and how to staff them, and state the cost. Because so much of your income from franchising comes up front, you will be able to fund these positions as needed.

Finally, there's the matter of integrity. For some uninformed or unscrupulous operators, franchising has been a "fast buck" vehicle. Just come up with a good-sounding idea and sell franchises! Lots of them! P. T. Barnum once said, "there's a sucker born every minute!" Let's dispel that postulate before we go any further. Franchising is not about a hunt for suckers, collecting fees, handing out manuals, providing a week or two of training, sending them off and then waiting for the royalty checks to come in. It's about understanding that you are going into a different business – a business in which you are expanding your company by carefully selecting "managers" with at least the same qualifications you would require to operate your own company-owned units. However, these "managers" will not only manage their businesses, they will own them. They will not be your employees; in a real sense, they will be your partners.

If you are not physically and mentally prepared to accept only highly qualified applicants, you and they will fail. Tempting as it is to take a check for $40,000 from a buyer when you really need the cash and payroll is on Friday, selling a franchise to an unqualified buyer is a recipe for failure. It immediately "poisons the well," because failed franchises scare away other prospective buyers. And in the long run it can lead to very nasty lawsuits. For more than thirty years, Francorp consultants have served as arbitrators, mediators and expert witnesses in more than eighty lawsuits involving franchise disputes. In most of these cases, defendant franchisors unscrupulously sold flawed concepts to unsuspecting buyers, sold franchises to unqualified buyers, or provided inadequate training and/or support to their franchisees. Ask yourself this question: "Would I hire as manager a person who knew nothing about my business, give him two or three weeks' training, hand him the keys to the business and take a six-month vacation?" We think not.

Selling a franchise is not unlike having a child. Your responsibility doesn't end with the birth. It begins there. With a child, you have a lifelong responsibility to grow, nurture, support, guide, and be involved. The same is true of a franchise for at least the term of the franchise agreement. The best companies are those who fully understand the necessity of recruitment, training and support. Companies like McDonald's, Culver's, and Midas have success statistics to validate this practice. Done right, franchising works well for everyone—franchisees, suppliers, consumers, and, not least, franchisors.

The Franchiseability Test

By now you should have some idea as to where your business stands in the spectrum between Totally Unfranchiseable and Eminently Franchiseable. But it may help you to get a more precise idea of your place along this spectrum by taking a brief quiz. Answer each of the following questions, add up your score and read the results below.

Points

1. Do you have an operating prototype?
No	1 point	
Yes	10 points	*10*

2. How many units do you have in operation?
Assign 1 point per unit up to 10.   *4*

3. How long since you first opened your business?
Not in operation yet	0 points	
Less than six months	2 points	
One year	4 points	
Two years	6 points	
Three years	8 points	
Four years or more	10 points	*10*

4. *To what degree is your business distinctive from its competitors?*

Not very	0 points	
Somewhat	3 points	
Very	7 points	
Unique	10 points	_3_

5. *How much would it cost to open one of your locations, not including franchise fees.*

$400,000 or more	2 points	
$200,000 to $399,000	4 points	
$100,000 to $199,000	6 points	
$50,000 to $99,000	8 points	
Less than $50,000	10 points	_2_

6. *The market for your business is:*

Local	0 points	
Regional	3 points	
National	8 points	
International	10 points	_8_

7. *Competition for the products or services you sell is:*

High	1 point	
Moderate	5 points	
Minimal	10 points	_5_

8. *How systematized is your business?*

Not very.	0	points
Some policies and/or handbooks.	2	points
Very well systematized and documented.	6	points
Highly systematized and computerized.	10	points 6

9. *How long would it take you to teach someone to operate your business?*

Special certification needed	1	point
2 to 6 months	2	points
1 to 2 months	4	points
1 to 3 weeks	7	points
1 week or less	10	points 4

10. *How do your sales compare with those of comparable businesses in your industry?*

Much lower	0	points
Somewhat lower	1	point
About the same	3	points
Somewhat higher	7	points
Much higher	10	points 3

Total points   55

Ratings

0 – 39 Time to step back and think about it. Your business needs to make significant strides – perhaps with the help of specialists in your industry – before franchising becomes a viable option. If a strong market for your business exists, look for ways to improve your score in other areas.

40 – 59 Fine tuning needed. You have made a promising beginning. Now is the time to work on areas critical to successful franchising, such as systematizing your business, boosting sales and adding elements that can make your business distinctive.

60 – 79 On the threshold. You have all of the elements in place for a successful franchise. At this point your own goals may be more of a determining factor as to whether or not you franchise than the viability of your business.

80 – 100 Look out McDonald's! There's no such thing as a Can't Miss Concept, but yours is about as close as a business can get to Total Franchiseability. Go for it!

Chapter 5

Getting Ready

We have talked at length about attributes that make a business franchiseable. But it will help you to appraise franchising and your place in it if you understand some general truths about this peculiar growth system before you enter into it.

Timing

In business, as in life, timing is everything. Enter a market that is not ready for your idea and you fail. Enter a market too late and a golden opportunity may be lost. Early computer companies anticipated the day when there would be a PC in every home. They revved up production…only to go bust. They were ten years too early. Several companies were already testing miniature portable radios with earphones when Akio Morita, chairman of Sony, boldly rushed into the market with Walkman, without field testing, focus groups, or market studies. He captured a new market at just the right moment. Whether or not the timing is right for your business is something to think about.

Quick vs. slick

Competition is also important. If you plan to compete in a market where a few companies dominate, you'd better be slick. We mentioned the burger market, where McDonald's, Burger King and Wendy's have a 72 percent market share. If you want to compete, you should have several very professional-looking units in operation, each of them highly organized with all systems perfected. You should also have extensive financial resources. After all, if you can't match the buying power, advertising, field support, R&D, and market visibility of your competitors they may very well eat you alive.

Which is not to say that you have no chance against them. There are many examples of companies that have taken on the "big boys" – and won! Wendy's came along when everyone said there wasn't room for another burger operation. But Wendy's used fresh ground beef, while everyone else used frozen hamburger patties. Wendy's was "hot and juicy," making burgers to order. And their "Where's the beef?" campaign illustrated their point of difference and helped them to elbow their way into the burger market, replacing the "Big Two" with the "Big Three."

Later, Jimmy Johns took on Subway and others by advertising "fresher and higher quality" ingredients and using the slogan, "Your mom wants you to eat here." In a few short years, Jimmy Johns went from one to 1000 units and to this day is the only franchisor to run full-page ads showing unit sales and profits.

On the other hand, if you are competing in a market that has no leaders with a significant market share – what we call a fragmented market – then it is more important to be quick. You don't have to be perfect – just be there first, fast, and before the competition. Kentucky Fried Chicken was the first major chicken chain, Midas the first muffler chain, Holiday Inn the first motel chain, Century 21 the first real estate chain. All had flaws at the beginning, but when you are first you have time to work out the flaws.

So be sure you are ready before you compete with "the big guys." But if you are lucky enough to be in one of those fragmented sectors where no names stand out, and if your business has a new twist, don't dilly-dally. Rocking chairs are full of people who coulda, shoulda, woulda if only they had acted, but instead froze at the switch. It's a tough call. To move or not to move? That is the question. It's gut-check time.

Small can be saleable

Whether your method is slick, quick, or neither, you'll benefit if the cost of getting into your business is low. The greater the franchisee's investment, the more potential buyers you exclude. Service businesses and home-based businesses usually cost less to own, but so do small retail businesses that allow a franchise to go into a 1,000 to 2,000 square foot store space with minimal leasehold improvements. Low tech is also desirable. Businesses that are simple to operate are easier to sell than those that require extensive training or certification that takes months to obtain.

Bad trends and good

Be careful of becoming identified with a celebrity or personality. Pepsi used Michael Jackson as a symbol, until he had legal problems. Jerry Lewis and Minnie Pearl were the figureheads for theater and chicken franchises that came to a bad end. Kenny Rogers' Chicken also tanked. Fads are also dangerous. There's just not much of a market anymore for hula-hoop stores.

Then there's the Bandwagon Syndrome, a vehicle that looks so good people jump on before it proves itself. Frozen yogurt stores, for example, opened across the country, but soon closed when they failed to make a profit. On the other hand lifestyle businesses, if they catch on, can be blockbusters—and, indeed, Blockbusters was one. But Starbucks is the poster child for lifestyle businesses. It's not about the coffee. It's about the ambience, the cache, and the cool. But let's face it, it sells. Curves, the no frills women's workout operation, does a counter-culture play on lifestyle. It's now cooler to go there than to high-priced Spandex-perfect environments of the chic health clubs.

Apply the polish

But back to the business you own, not the one you might wish for. If you have a physical location, retail or otherwise, it must be made attractive, neat, and appealing to a prospective franchise buyer. Remember, first impressions are important to people who are about to quit their jobs, refinance their homes, and are looking at several potential franchises. They really have no way to evaluate which franchise is going to be the best fit, the most profitable, offer the most services, and provide the best chance for success. That's because few franchises make earnings claims in their Disclosure Documents. Prospects judge the franchisor based upon what they see and hear. The franchisor with the most persuasive brochure, most comprehensive web site, most engaging salesman, and most attractive place of business often gets the sale. So, if that's the game you're going to be in, you'd better understand how to play it. Start with décor and graphics, but don't neglect documents, operations manuals, brochures, DVDs, CD ROMs, computers and software. Observable, tangible elements are integral to your sales presentation. You might be an intelligent, funny, and interesting person, but if you show up at a black tie event in overalls, you may not get the chance to display all that charm.

Remember how you got here

Granted, franchising is a very different business than the one you're used to. Take just one example. The average sale in your business may be anywhere from $25 to $2,500. When you offer to sell a franchise, your buyer is likely to need between $150,000 to $500,000 in cash! If we come into your place of business, cause no trouble and pay for your goods or services, we are considered good customers even if we are complete idiots. But if you sell a franchise to a buyer who offers you a check but lacks the necessary qualifications to operate your business, you will rue the day. If they fail, that negative effect can cause other potential buyers to shy away from your franchise offering. Franchise buyers are like deer in the forest – if they hear a twig snap, they are gone.

Don't allow the size of the sale to influence you. Go back to what made you successful. Hold to the basic principles that built your business: integrity, hard work, good marketing, and knowing and taking care of your customers and employees. Plus, exercising good judgment generally. Your goal is to propagate your company culture, not to lose it.

Get the help you need

We have stressed that franchising is a different business from the one you are now in. For that reason, it will almost certainly be necessary to obtain professional help in creating a franchise entity. Indeed, if the name of your business is Jones Products, Inc. you will most certainly need a new corporation to run the franchise program, say Jones Products Franchise, Inc.

But even before that happens, you may want to obtain advice about the franchise marketplace. What are today's franchise buyers looking for? How much do they have to spend? Who else is selling franchises like yours? You'll learn quickly enough that companies selling franchises for the same type of business as yours are not necessarily your principal competitors. You are competing with everyone who has a booth at that franchise show and everyone who has a franchise ad in a newspaper or magazine or is listed on a web site.

For these and many other reasons, it is important to have your Business Plan developed or, at a minimum, reviewed by professionals. A CPA can tell you if your plan is financially viable and help you to determine the amount of capital you will need to commit to the project. An attorney, preferably a franchise attorney, can inform you of the legal requirements for incorporating, registering your trade name, franchise compliance, and other legal issues. A franchise consultant can tell you if your business is even franchiseable and can assist you in developing the business plan, legal documents, operation manuals, marketing strategies and materials, and guide you through the process. But be sure to get references before you sign on the dotted line.

Finding money

In Chapter 2 we described various methods of raising funds for expansion, pointing out that franchising is indeed one of them and can outshine them all. But the capital that franchising provides goes primarily to the growth of your franchise system. Even if you do choose to franchise, you may need additional capital for such projects as opening company-owned stores or offices, adding computers, a web site, staff, inventory or new elements to your existing business. Here are some options:

Venture Capital

If your company is substantial and you decide to pursue venture capital, it's a good idea to know what you're getting into. Here is what venture capital firms are looking for:

1. **A capital infusion of minimally $1,000,000.** They don't usually do smaller deals.

2. **A well-articulated Business Plan** – not an inch-thick document loaded with statistics, but a compact presentation that includes an executive summary. The concept, the company, the management, the market, the competition, and the strategy must be concisely described. An assessment of capital needed and its use, plus a 5-year cash flow analysis, must be included. With a well-done, clearly articulated Business Plan, you at least have a shot. Without it, you don't.

3. **Strong management.** There is no shortage of good ideas. Venture capital firms look for a CEO and a management team that have managed their company successfully through strong and impressive growth. They want to know that you are capable of managing the monster you are liable

to create with the infusion of substantial capital. They also want to know how you and your management team will look in a Disclosure Document. Have you ever managed a public company or taken a company public? Have you ever done a deal involving investors, and how did it work out?

4. **Personnel needs.** If you have gaps in your management team, your Business Plan must clearly describe the type of people you will need, such as a financial person or Internet expert, and your plan to bring them in.

5. **Deliberate planning.** Define each stage of expansion and state its cost. You are not likely to get the entire million at once. Show that Phase I will require, say, $400,000, and that when it is complete Phase II will cost $600,000. Phase in your additional staff and hard assets. State that you plan to bring the CFO on board in month six and add the Christmas inventory in month ten.

6. **An understanding of the way venture capital firms structure their deals.** Percentage of ownership is not usually a vital factor. They are looking for 50 to 70 percent annual return on their investment, regardless of what percentage of ownership

they have. They want an *exit strategy* that gets them out in three to five years, tops. That may be acceptable to you if you are giving 10 percent of your company in the process. If you must give 80 percent of your company, it may not. But regardless of their percentage of ownership, if you fail to make your projections, they will have the right to take over your company. They may have other requirements as well. They may want a Revenue Participation Warrant (a percentage of your gross sales) off the top. Or, in return for their million dollars they may want their one million in equity treated as half equity and half loan, which needs to be paid back with interest.

If you decide to seek venture capital, control will be an issue. No matter what percentage a venture capital firm acquires, they will have a major role in all strategic or financial decisions. This often presents a conflict between entrepreneurs used to "calling their own shots" and making quick decisions and venture capitalists who want to minimize expenses to position the company for a sale.

Be realistic about your chances. According to a survey in USA Today, only 3,400 venture capital deals were done in the US in 2006. Considering that there are 20 million small businesses (to say nothing of large ones), the percentage is minuscule. Be careful of consultants who want a fee to help you acquire venture capital. Ask for the names of companies for whom they have helped to get funds and call them.

Finally, give yourself a deadline and have your Plan B ready. If venture capital is not forthcoming by a specific date, launch it. Otherwise you can spend years chasing your financial tail.

Equity funding

Businesses that seek equity funding are willing to exchange a share of their company, either in the form of a partnership, limited partnership, or for shares of stock in exchange for needed capital. While venture capital is the first kind of equity funding that usually comes to mind, there are other sources you may choose to consider. You might, for example, find a partner who is willing to invest in your company in return for a share of it. Many such people want a job in the company, which can work well if the person has skills that are needed. Some entrepreneurs are great at ideas, marketing and sales, but not so good at finance, accounting, or organization tasks. That kind of partner can be useful.

Another equity finance option is the private placement, a private offering to a limited number of sophisticated investors, called accredited investors. To make a private placement you will need to create a private placement memorandum, which is similar to the prospectus required for an Initial Public Offering. Only a few entrepreneurs with substantial businesses and strong track records can opt for IPOs. If either of these last two options are a consideration, RUN, don't walk, to your nearest securities lawyer. A psychiatrist might also be a good idea!

Debt financing

Debt financing, or borrowing money, is also an option for expanding your company. Typically, for starters, you will go to your current bank with your Business Plan in hand, and talk to a loan officer. If you have already borrowed money there and have a good payment record, you have an excellent chance of getting the loan, MAYBE. The "maybe" comes into play because no matter how wonderful your track record is with the bank or how well drafted and articulated your Business Plan, it all comes down to collateral. What is your net worth, business and personal, because banks will almost always require a personal guarantee on a loan. The other factor is the bank's loan ratio, which is usually 2 to 1, or even 1 to 1. This means that if you have a net worth of $100,000, the bank will probably lend you $100,000 or $200,000 at most. They will also usually require that your financial statements be audited by a CPA and that your real estate be appraised. Some banks are tied in with the SBA (Small Business Administration) and can go as high as 4 to 1, or even 5 to 1, lending ratios. They are "indirect SBA lenders." You can also go directly to the SBA. For more information, contact your local bank or the SBA.

Other options

If you need to buy or build buildings, money is generally fairly easy to obtain. Ten to 20 percent down payments usually get the job done with conventional mortgages. Typically, if you buy the land for cash you can usually leverage it into a construction loan, and then it's a 20- or 30-year mortgage.

Equipment financing is also fairly easy to obtain, especially if you are using "off the shelf" equipment, fixtures, computers, machines, or vehicles. Financing companies view standard brands as collateral and readily marketable should they have to repossess them. Financing for customized equipment, on the other hand, is more difficult to obtain. Equipment financing is done at a substantially higher rate of interest than business or real estate loans and generally for a five- to seven - year period.

Receivables financing or "factoring" receivables may also be an option. In fact, some finance companies specialize in receivables financing. If a sizable amount of your assets is tied up in receivables from customers, you can pledge your receivables as collateral and borrow as much as 80 percent of their value.

Then, of course, there's always Aunt Martha. She may be willing to lend you money at 3 or 4 percent more than she is receiving at her local savings and loan. Of course, it's one thing to put yourself at risk and another to put Aunt Martha's life savings at risk. Be careful.

Many entrepreneurs and franchisees refinance their homes to establish, expand, franchise or buy franchises. A low interest, 30-year payback loan takes a lot of pressure off of a newly formed business enterprise.

Financing for franchisees

Now that we've explored some finance options for you as a franchisor, let's look at the financing needs of the franchise buyers we want to attract. The sale of a franchise almost always requires that a buyer obtain financing of some type. Moreover, the franchisee may need financing from more than one source. Some financial institutions limit transactions to real estate, others to equipment, and others to receivables. Some limit them to specific types of businesses, such as restaurants, or avoid specific businesses (such as restaurants). Fortunately, in recent years franchised businesses have been identified as generally attractive, irrespective of type, by financial institutions. As a result, companies like Franchise Finance Corporation, General Electric Credit Corporation and Francorp Capital were formed to put all of these finance needs under one roof.

In most cases, the sale of your franchises will hinge less upon total price than upon how much cash up front is needed. Therefore, it is incumbent upon you, the franchisor, to line up financing sources before you offer franchises for sale. The prospective buyer from another city who seeks financing locally may be turned down because their bank or finance company doesn't know you. It could cost you the sale. To avoid such problems, you can, if you have the money, provide financing yourself. If you don't, you may want to work with a company like the three named above to obtain single-source financing for all your franchisees' needs.

* * *

In one respect, franchising is not so different from any other type of endeavor – business or otherwise. The better prepared you are, the greater your chance of success. In the next few chapters we will go into detail about specific preparations you must make to create your franchise program.

Chapter 6

Determining Your Franchise Structure

For the business owner who has decided
1. that his or her business is appropriate for franchising,
2. that the franchise market is right for that business,
3. that he or she is ready for the challenges of franchising, and
4. that franchising from a financial stand-point is the right way to go, there is just one step left: putting the franchise together.

At one time that was a no-brainer, or seemed to be. In the early days of franchising, on through the explosive 1950s and 60s, when new franchises were popping up everywhere, the process was simple. Put up a sign in your store and an ad in the paper offering franchises for sale. Find someone to pay you a franchise fee.

Draw up some kind of document providing for certain services in return for the fee and ongoing royalties. Sign on the dotted line. That was it. You were a franchisor.

Two things happened to change that pattern. The first was competition. Franchises that had started on a shoestring without much planning faltered and died. Both franchisors and franchisees got hurt in the process. The second thing that happened was partly a result of these failures, but primarily the result of publicity about the occasional unscrupulous franchisor. In some cases franchisors took the franchise fees and vanished. In others, franchisors failed to give proper training or support to franchisees. In 1971, California became the first state to regulate franchising. Twenty-two other states followed during the Seventies. Then, in 1978 the Federal Government decreed that all states must regulate franchising. With the increasing sophistication of franchising practices in recent years, coupled with the need to comply with state and federal regulations, the process of putting together a franchise program has changed significantly. Today, a new franchisor eager to get off on the right foot will take five basic steps in creating a franchise program:

1. Determine the structure
2. Create the legal documents
3. Develop operating manuals
4. Devise a marketing plan
5. Implement a sales strategy

We will discuss each of these steps at length in the coming chapters. But the place to start is with structure. Until you decide what kind of franchises you want to sell – to whom, where, and for how much – everything else is premature. The amount of thought and knowledge you bring to the making of these decisions can be critical to the success of your franchise program.

The type of franchise

In many respects, the type of franchise you sell will depend upon the nature of your business. If you want to bring existing businesses of the same type as yours into an expanding organization, a la Century 21, a conversion franchise is your only option. And if you do become a conversion franchisor, you may want to franchise rapidly by selling the rights to convert existing businesses to subfranchisors. If, on the other hand, your business is of a type that can be replicated for a low cost and is simple to operate, you may want to consider multi-unit (or area development) franchising, allowing well-financed individuals or companies to develop an entire market on a pre-determined schedule. But if yours is like most new franchises, whether or not you opt later for rapid expansion techniques, you will first sell individual franchises.

Here is a summary of the pros and cons for each type of franchise:

Pros	Cons
Individual Franchise	
• Builds a strong company foundation	• Less sophisticated owners
• Owner operator	• Limited capital
• Furnishes own capital	• More training required
• Will do it your way	• More support required
• Faster saturation in market	• Slower growth
Area Development	
• Faster growth	• Can't get sophisticated buyers until you are bigger
• More sophisticated operators	• Heavier up-front expenditures
• Capitalizes on window of opportunity	• Can create a monster you can't manage
• Locks out competition	• Requires larger more complex infrastructure
• Gets there first	• Rapid growth exposes weaknesses in system
	• Slower saturation in a given market.
Subfranchising	
• Faster growth	• Quality control-sensitive businesses may suffer
• *Only* way to expand with low volume businesses	• Relegates screening of prospective franchisees to a third party
• Sales people pay *you* to sell your franchises	• Relegates field support of franchises to a third party
• Solves field support costs	

As this list suggests, you should be careful about starting an area development program. You may want to sell large territories to affluent buyers, but such people have a way of showing up with lawyers and accountants and asking annoying questions like: "How long have you been in business? How profitable are your units? How many are already in operation? Can I see the financials?" If you're not ready for such questions, it's better to sell individual franchises first, establish several profitable units, and begin building a strong franchise organization capable of handling rapid growth and sophisticated franchisees. Besides, once you have successfully developed a number of individual franchisees in one geographical market, you will have in fact created the prototype for an area development. At that point, you'll be happy to answer such questions. Finally, an area development strategy may actually result in slower development in specific markets because area developers typically build one unit in the first year, two in the second and so on. If, instead, you "spike" a given market with one unit and properly advertise you may be able to sell ten more within a year.

Individual franchises

And that is what most new franchisors do. They create a program designed to sell franchises to individual owners for one physical location or one territory, depending upon the type of business. As we noted earlier, a restaurant, muffler shop, beauty salon, or hotel operates at a physical location. A franchise that involves temporary office placement, carpet cleaning, the sale of industrial products, or accounting services requires a general territory with a population large enough to support the business.

Even if you choose to sell individual rather than area development franchises, you will probably be wise to select a *market saturation* strategy over a *market penetration* strategy. Market penetration is designed to get you into a lot of cities one franchise at a time, but unless these franchises do exceptionally high sales volumes and contribute huge amounts in royalties, you will go broke trying to service them. For this reason, we recommend clustering individual franchise units in one market before going on to the next. By opening five, ten, or even 100 units in a city you benefit by economies of scale in purchasing and advertising and – most importantly – *saturate* the market. Franchising is a saturation strategy. Scorched earth. A unit everywhere we can possibly have one as long as the market will support it. We have to acknowledge the fact that every unit is not going to be a home run. Some units will generate huge sales and others minimal. The key is to be sure that we don't establish a unit in a market that cannot be profitable.

This said, it is not always easy for a new franchisor to achieve market saturation. One client of ours, Panda Express, was a mall-based business. We recommended that they also go into on-the-street or strip-center locations to fill in the market. They did so and thus were able to justify support costs.

Granted, there are times when market penetration is justified. A temporary employment business, for example, might require only one franchise for an entire city. In such cases, the franchise fee would vary depending upon the size of the market: $35,000 for Des Moines, perhaps, and $200,000 for Cleveland. But don't sell a large territory to a franchisee who intends to develop it over a period of years. The buyer should have adequate resources to saturate the market with inventory, services and advertising. Taking a check for $100,000 from a franchise buyer only to discover a year later that very little business is being done in that market is not the way to run a franchise.

Multi-unit franchises

If your business is both substantial and sophisticated, a multi-unit franchise strategy can be the most effective way to dominate the market. Multiple unit buyers tend to be well capitalized and highly experienced business operators. Many hold more than one franchise, especially in the same general field. An owner of ten KFC's, for example, might also own ten Taco Bells because they are not competing concepts. When Pepsi Cola acquired KFC, Taco Bell and Pizza Hut, it spun them off in a leveraged management buyout to a group that took that business public, calling it originally Tricon and subsequently changing the name to Yum. Since that transaction, the Yum Group has been consolidating units so that a single franchisee can have a Taco Bell, a KFC and Pizza Hut under one roof. It is a brilliant strategy also used by Allied Domecq in the co-branding of their brands Dunkin' Donuts, Baskin Robbins and Togo's. If you're in the restaurant business and are considering area development franchising, look into MUFSO, (Multi-Unit Food Service Operators). It is a group of hundreds of companies, many of whom have multiple concepts of multiple units, that meets annually. At these meetings they share techniques and success stories. They also shop for additional multiple unit concepts to add in their markets, thereby making even better use of centralized administrative services, commissaries, payroll, purchasing, etc. Many also have additional land next to existing restaurant operations, capable of accommodating new concepts. Similar bundling has been done by retailers, automotive companies, and service businesses. Service Master, for example, acquired personal service businesses such as Terminex (pest control), Trugreen (lawn control) and Merry Maids (maid services) that cater to the same customers.

Subfranchisors

For a low-cost business (minimal investment and annual sales of $150,000 or less) that decides to use a market saturation strategy, subfranchising can be the answer – and may be the only one. You would select markets capable of establishing, say, twenty or more individual franchises, then sell to sales-oriented individuals or companies in those markets the right to establish a predetermined number of franchises. The subfranchisor would receive both a percentage of the franchisee fee and a percentage of the ongoing royalties from each franchise sold in his or her territory. In addition to making the sale, the subfranchisor will assume the responsibility of servicing franchisees. The point is, of course, that you as a franchisor would have a hard time making monthly visits to franchises in another city that paid royalties of at most, say, $10,000

(10 percent of gross sales of $100,000) a year. But you might have no difficulty providing through a sub-franchisor services such as advertising, new products, etc. for a percentage of that amount. Because the sub franchisor is based in the market where the franchises are sold, half (if that is the percentage you agree upon) the franchise fee and half the royalties for each franchise are sufficient to pay for the cost of sales efforts and servicing. Of course, sub-franchisors, like franchisees, do need your periodic attention. Your agreement must compensate you for making periodic (monthly) visits. Granted, you get a smaller percentage of the pie. But that is the basic principal of franchising: the sacrifice of total ownership and control of something small for partial ownership and control of something large. The principle of shared responsibility – franchisor and subfranchisor – has made subfranchising a popular strategy for low volume businesses. One caveat, however: it is generally not a good idea to use subfranchising as an expansion strategy in quality-control sensitive businesses like restaurant operations.

The franchisee profile

You'll do well to decide in advance what type of person you want to own your franchise. That decision, in the case of mult-unit franchisees and subfranchisors, will not be difficult. Both are defined to a large extent by the nature of the business. Mult-unit franchisees must be affluent and highly experienced in business. Subfranchisors must be, to begin with, excellent sales people.

Individual franchisees are another matter. For one thing, they are likely to have less money and less business experience. But, as we noted earlier, if there is a single benchmark for an individual franchisee, it is this: He or she should be the same type of person you would hire if you were opening another branch and seeking a manager. Like managers, individual franchise owners should have leadership, sales, and people skills, as well as physical stamina and job experience. Unlike managers, they will put up the capital as well. When the time comes to select franchise applicants, don't be shy about asking for detailed personal information such as school transcripts. It is our experience that ideally you are seeking A students. A students often work for companies managed by B students owned by C students. You do not want the person who likes to "wing it." Nor do you want an entrepreneur eager to put his or her stamp on everything. Most A student candidates will have worked in structured environments for relatively long periods of time. They will tend to be comfortable following rules and regulations. A good franchise prospect will have held jobs for at least three or four years and will have had several promotions. It's helpful if the applicant has been married for a long time (it shows they can withstand pain). And indeed, individuals who have withstood the ups and downs of business and personal relationships stand a good chance of being successful franchisees. Check their driving record. Not only the tendency to speed and break other laws but alcohol or drug problems will show up. Check their credit record. Prospects who fail to make credit card or mortgage payments and other commitments on a timely basis may not pay their royalties on time either. Ask what their life is like. A person who takes the 6:00 a.m. train to work every day, returns home at 6:00 p.m., eats dinner, watches TV and goes to bed, then on weekends "chills out," is probably not a good candidate for a franchise. You want candidates who bowl on Monday nights, coach little league on Tuesday nights, serve on a church committee on Wednesday nights and on weekends are active with their families in the community. Your franchisees will have to hire, train and motivate employees, interface with customers, vendors, and community organizations, unload boxes, be on their feet for long periods of time, and work long hours. We all go through this in building our own businesses; and any franchise, even though it is well defined, will still require this kind of commitment to make it work.

One rule you should absolutely observe creating a franchisee profile is this: *Never sell a franchise to an absentee owner.* Absentee ownership defeats the very purpose of franchising. It adds an extra layer of expense while diminishing its principal advantage: motivation. Owner-operators are the backbone of franchising.

Territories

In addition to making decisions about your type of franchise, growth strategy and prospective franchisee, you will need to consider the matter of territory. Should you, for example, give your franchisee an exclusive territory? We say not if you can help it. Territories that can sustain one unit today may easily accept three or more within a few years. Not only do populations change, so do business patterns, new product offerings, shopping patterns, and surrounding environments. There is a danger, however, for franchisors who provide no exclusive territory. In their eagerness to achieve market saturation they may encroach in areas perceived by franchisees as their own market. Such encroachment has given rise to a number of nasty franchisor/franchisee disputes.

If your business is of a certain type – sales offices and mobile units are examples – you may need to protect the territory of your franchisees because the practices of competitors or the demands of franchisees require it. This may also be true of businesses with locations that attract customers or from which deliveries originate. In such cases, we generally recommend that the franchisor assign an Area of Primary Responsibility (APR) to each franchisee. APRs tend to be smaller than the economic market surrounding a unit. Moreover, the franchisee may sell products and services to customers in another franchisee's APR so long as the customer initiates contact. This allows franchisees with the most effective sales and marketing program to build business through referrals.

During the sales process, some franchisors sweeten the pot for franchisees by offering the "right of first refusal" or an "option" on an adjacent territory. We do not recommend this practice. Franchisees have a way of exercising their option only after you have spent months of hard work getting a prospect to agree to buy the adjacent area. The best way to deal with a franchisee who wants the rights to an adjacent territory is to require a deposit of half the franchise fee for that additional market with the stipulation that the franchisee open that unit within a specified period of time – usually one year – or lose the deposit.

Services

You should determine as much as you can in advance what services you will offer franchisees and what their cost will be. Training, of course, is essential. As a new franchisor you will probably not need a special training facility or classroom. You may, however, want to create a training schedule to assure that nothing is missed. Frankly, the best training you can provide is to have the franchisee work for you for a month or two and become intimately involved in all aspects of your business. You meet with them at 7:00 in the morning to discuss the day's activity and they help you turn the key to close the place at 11:00 p.m. The reality is, however, that most franchises settle for three or four weeks. On the average, we estimate the cost of training a franchisee at $2000 to $3000.

If the location of your business is important to generating customer traffic, you may want to assist your franchisee in finding a suitable site. Typically, as a first step, the franchisor provides each franchisee with a list of site criteria. Among these criteria might be population density within a specific radius; income, age and buying patterns of this population group; traffic patterns near the location; and preferred types of businesses in the area. Normally, the franchisee will take the list to a real estate broker, who in turn will suggest several available sites that best fit the list. Once the franchisee has selected the site that best meets these criteria, he or she will submit a description of the site for the franchisor's approval. Even in cases where location is not vital to customer traffic, the franchisor may have suggestions as to the preferred type of business establishment, market characteristics and location within the franchisee's territory. We estimate the cost of such services at between $1000 and $2000.

You will, of course, be sending someone to the franchisee's place of business for a period of time before and after the business opens. Who will go and how much time that person will spend depends in part upon the complexity of the business and in part upon how much prior training the franchisee has received. The purpose is, of course, to help the franchisee get a running start. You will probably spend between $3000 and $5000 per franchise on these services.

There could be other services specific to your franchise. Some franchisors do the billing for their franchisees or process the work. In the case of marketing companies specializing in coupon mailings where franchisees sign up advertisers and collect the fees, the franchisor often prints and mails the coupons to residents in the franchisees' markets and remits a commission on any sales to the franchisees. Some franchisors in the healthcare business bill the government on behalf of franchisees for Medicaid reimbursement. In such cases extra fees must be built into the franchise program. You can either bill the franchisee directly for such services or, if the service will be fairly standardized from franchisee to franchisee, add a percentage that you think will cover them to the royalty you charge.

Franchise marketing and sales

Think about this: If the first ten buyers of your franchise do not succeed, neither will your franchise program. Your franchise marketing and sales program must be planned accordingly. Some franchises hire outside brokers to handle franchise sales. We don't recommend it, especially at the beginning. All the evidence we've seen suggests that franchise sales should be made directly by the franchisor. We discussed earlier the process of qualifying, interviewing and checking out franchise prospects. The closer you are personally to that process, the better the result will be. This is not to say that you shouldn't at some point employ a sales person for that purpose. But it's critical that your sales program be driven not by commissions but by the standards you set for a qualified franchisee. For purposes of setting the franchise fee, we suggest that between $4000 and $6000 be allocated for franchise sales expenses. You'll need a similar amount to create and place ads aimed at generating franchise sales leads.

Franchise Fee

Having assessed the tasks listed above, you are ready to decide on a franchise fee, the up-front payment you receive from a franchisee that is designed to compensate you for all those services. To help you determine your franchise fee, the following chart illustrates typical high-end and low-end franchisor expenses:

Expenses Per Franchisee

	LOW	HIGH
Marketing and Lead Generation Expenses	$3,000	$6,000
Sales Expense	$4,000	$6,000
Site Evaluation	$1,000	$2,000
General & Administrative Expenses	$1,000	$3,000
Headquarters Training	$2,000	$3,000
On-Site Training and Travel	$3,000	$4,000
X-factor: Initial Support	$3,000	$5,000
ANTICIPATED COST PER SALE	**$17,000**	**$29,000**

Note the term "X-factor." It's normal at the beginning of the franchisor/franchisee relationship to schedule a visit to the franchisee on a weekly basis. Depending upon the distances involved, these visits can range from moderately costly to very expensive. As time goes on, of course, you will visit less often. We recommend that your representative be present for one to two weeks at the opening of the franchise, once a week during the first quarter, every other week during the second quarter, every third week during the third quarter and monthly in the fourth quarter. For restaurant, retail, child-related, pet-related and similar franchises, visits will continue to be monthly thereafter. For many others they can be quarterly.

If you draw a line representing the cost of these visits over time, it will look like this:

While expenses go from high to low, revenue takes an opposite course. The following line represents royalty revenue to the franchisor from the franchisee.

At the beginning it is low, and as time goes on it grows. When we cross the two lines we have what we call the X-factor, thus:

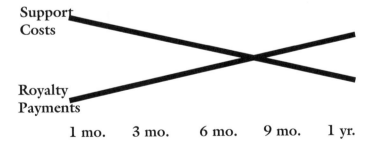

Support
Costs

Royalty
Payments

1 mo.   3 mo.   6 mo.   9 mo.   1 yr.

As this chart shows, about seven months after the franchise has opened, revenue from the franchisee will begin to exceed your expenses. How do you support your franchise program until that happens? Answer:with a portion of your franchise fees. Looking again at the chart entitled "Expenses Per Franchisee," we would usually recommend that companies at the low end charge a franchise fee in the range of $25,000 to $35,000. It's worth noting that some new franchises charge even lower fees. Curves, the physical fitness for women franchise, set an unusually low franchise fee of $20,000 and between 1995 and 2003 established 6733 units! On the other hand, some companies charge initial franchise fees of up to $250,000, depending upon the economics and profitability of the business.

Royalties

The royalty, of course, is the ongoing percentage you receive of the franchisee's gross sales—before expenses and before profits. It is the payment you get for the continued use of your name and business system. A study our company made with DePaul University some years back concluded that the average royalty for the 900 franchises we surveyed was 6 percent. Nothing we've seen since would lead us to revise that figure. Still, royalties do vary from franchise to franchise.

Three factors will weigh heavily upon the royalty you select. One is competition. If there are businesses similar to yours in the franchise marketplace, what are they charging? It can pay to find out. The second and most important factor is affordability. Remember your franchisee needs to make a manager's salary plus a minimum of 15 percent return on invested capital. Can they afford to pay 6 percent? 10 percent? 4 percent? Typically, service businesses can afford to pay higher percentages because their expenses are lower. But so are their gross sales. Businesses selling products with narrow margins will have higher sales levels but will pay smaller percentages. If you have been in business for a number of years, you should have little trouble determining what percentage of sales a franchisee can afford to pay and still make a profit. At the same time, if you have had no experience in franchising you will be less qualified to judge what you will need in royalty income to provide services needed by your franchisees. The third factor is expenses. How often must you visit each franchise? Who will you send? What will be their salaries, car expenses, airfares, and hotel costs? You may want to consult professionals with franchise experience to assist with estimates.

One more word about royalties. We often joke that we collect them weekly because it is inconvenient to collect them hourly. Actually, weekly collections benefit both franchisor and franchisee. Franchisor gets the money needed to operate on a timely basis. Franchisee is spared a big hit at the end of each month. Monthly collections, on the other hand, can pose a real problem for everyone. If a franchisee is delinquent in sending weekly royalties, the franchisor will know it quickly and be able to respond. Sometimes such delinquencies are a symptom of problems that can be corrected if the franchisor learns of them quickly. If royalties are collected on a monthly basis, they are not due until the first week of the following month and it's very easy to have a franchisee two months in arrears before a red flag goes up. To minimize collection problems even more, you should consider requiring payment of royalties by EFT (Electronic Fund Transfer) rather than the traditional check. This new process eliminates all sorts of transaction problems and expenses related to paper, and gives you immediate notice of non-payment difficulties.

Advertising requirements

You will want to give thought in advance to the subject of advertising. How much will you do on behalf of your franchisees? How much will they be expected to do on their own? Usually the franchisor helps the franchisee advertise in two ways. Early in the franchise program the franchisor will provide in-store ads, print ads, mailers and commercials that have worked for the company in the past. As time goes on, the franchisor will create new advertising as well. In addition, when the franchise reaches a certain size the franchisor will place regional or national advertising designed to benefit all franchisees. For all of these activities, franchisors generally charge an advertising fee to franchisees of between 1 percent and 1.5 percent of gross sales.

A word of caution, however. Businesses that have been operating for years sometimes grow comfortable. If most of your income is generated from repeat business, you may have forgotten what it takes to start from scratch, when no one knows your name or who you are. A franchisee of this kind of business will have just such a challenge: carving out an identity in a new market. As a franchisor, one of your tasks will be to provide the advertising materials that will enable the franchisee to do just that. And that is true whether your franchisee will have a high-traffic corner location or is located in an enclosed mall and is captive to the traffic that the mall generates. When Sears has a sale, everybody does business. But how can your franchisee stimulate business on other days?

All of which gets us to the second role of the franchisor: overseeing local advertising. If your franchisees need to attract customers to their locations, you will probably want to require that each one spend a specific minimal amount for their Grand Opening. The typical new business starts with a "soft opening" for a month or two while the business trains employees, gets used to traffic patterns, makes adjustments on equipment, product offerings, pricing, and attains a comfort level. The Grand Opening blitz itself can consist of print ads, television commercials, radio commercials, Internet activity, banners, etc., depending upon the nature of the business and the size of its market. Many franchisors require that a franchisee set aside between $5,000 and $10,000 for their Grand Opening blitz.

You will probably also want to require that your franchisees spend a minimal amount against a percentage of sales for ongoing local advertising. One thousand dollars per month or 4 percent of sales, whichever is greater, is frequently stipulated. This must be spent on company-approved advertising programs. Some franchisors prescribe "gorilla advertising" programs for franchises that open an isolated unit in a new market. In lieu of expensive television, radio and newspaper ads, they resort to flyers for car windshields, door-hangers at residences, coupon mailings or promotions with other businesses in their area. A franchisor will be challenged continually to come up with fresh advertisements, commercials and other promotional materials that franchisees can employ using their own advertising dollars.

There is yet a third advertising function to be considered as your franchise grows: cooperative advertising. Most franchise agreements require that at such time as there are two or more operating units in the same media market, the franchisor has the right to require the franchisees to pool their money into a cooperative advertising fund, which the franchisor usually administers. That pool of money is used strictly to buy ad space, TV or radio time or Internet visibility. Indeed, cooperative Internet advertising has become critical for some businesses. Because of the art of search engine optimization and the need to purchase "key words" (see page 160), you may need to require monthly contributions by franchisees to your web site development, web site maintenance, and Internet advertising fund.

Great care must be taken in the management of your cooperative advertising fund. Some administrative, production, consulting and professional charges can be levied against it, but this very visible fund will require quarterly and annual reporting of exactly how those monies are applied. A large number of the more than eighty lawsuits in which we have testified as an expert witness dealt with how these funds were handled. Cooperative advertising can generate another kind of controversy as well. On the face of it, cooperative advertising is a simple concept. In actuality, it can be complicated because media costs differ enormously from market to market. When one group of franchisees contributes to a fund and is able to get frequent television exposure because media costs in its market are low, while another group of franchisees in a higher cost market spends the same amount of money and gets much less TV time, the second group will often complain. Unless the franchisor is in constant contact with franchisees to explain such anomalies, disputes can result.

As your franchise grows, we recommend that you form an ad council consisting of one franchisee representative from each market. Your ad council will meet quarterly. You may even ask the council to select the advertising agency for your franchise, after reviewing three or four agency presentations. By allowing the council to actively participate in approving the ad campaigns, you can eliminate a potential source of franchisee resentment should the campaign not succeed. Even large, sophisticated companies make bad guesses on advertising programs and an ad council can protect you from unpleasant consequences.

Term of Agreement

Finally, you will need to determine the length of your contract with your franchisees. Two factors are in play here. One is the size of the franchisee's investment. It is unreasonable to expect someone to make a large investment and get a short – one- to five-year – agreement. The second factor is your self-interest. So long as a franchise is performing well, you will want the franchise to be part of your program indefinitely. For these reasons most individual franchises are issued for a period of twenty years. However, to protect you in the event that changes in your franchise agreement become necessary, you will want to divide your twenty-year agreement into five-year increments. Franchisees have the option of renewing the agreement every five years, provided that they sign the then-current franchise agreement with its then-current terms. *Remember, you can terminate a franchisee at any time they are not operating in compliance with your quality and operating standards.*

* * *

Having considered all of these issues, thereby creating the structure of your franchise, your next step is to put the program together. In the next chapter we'll discuss how to start that process.

Making It Legal

When you franchise your business you will need two legal documents, a Franchise Agreement and a Disclosure Document. And to draft those documents you will need an attorney who specializes in franchise law. These lawyers track franchise laws, present and proposed, keep tabs on legislation and litigation involving franchising, and are familiar with the business issues relating to franchise operations.

What do you suppose will be the first question a franchise attorney will ask you? It's a good bet she or he will want to know whether you have formed a separate corporation to operate the franchise company. If you have not, you should do so. A separate corporation provides your existing business with a measure of protection from liability and is altogether a healthy way to create a franchise company. Your local attorney can do the job.

Registering your name

And what is the second question your franchise attorney will ask? Probably this: "Have you protected the name of your business through federal trademark registration?" In our experience most businesses seeking to franchise have not gone through this process. In fact, some business owners are surprised to learn that by recording their business name with the state at the time they incorporate they have done nothing, per se, to establish ownership of a trademark of their business name nor have they protected their rights to the name of their business.

Obtaining a federal trademark registration for your businesss is an important step in assuring that you have the right to use that name – a vital consideration when you franchise. After all, you are selling to the franchisee only two things: use of your name and your system of operation. And to sell the rights to use a name, it helps to own those rights. If you do not yet have an operating prototype – and thus proof of use of the name – registration of your name becomes even more important. In addition, of course, the simple use of the name of your business over time in a specific geographic area helps you to protect your rights to that name.

Lawyers tell us that getting a trademark registered is not particularly difficult, providing... And that's the key word: providing. Providing nobody else has already registered the same name or a similar name. Providing also that no other business using your name started using it before you did. And, finally, providing that under the law your name meets the requirements for federal trademark registration.

Let's start with the last of these "providings." Certain types of names will not be registered. If the name of your business is Joe's Appliances, it won't get registered. Too many Joes out there. Nor will it be registered if it's merely descriptive. Hot and Spicy Pizza may be what you're selling, but so are many others. Not a good name. But if your name is distinctive in some way (a coined word like Exxon or Google or Yahoo, for example), your chances are better. It should be mentioned that if your name is "borderline registrable"– a term we will not presume to define – it will help if it is used with a distinctive logo.

If an attorney knowledgeable about trademark law tells you that your name meets the government's qualifications for registration, then it's a good idea to have him or her conduct a search to determine whether anyone else has registered it or is using it. Trademark searches, like ice cream cones, come in various sizes. A cursory search, like a single dip cone, is the basic product. It will cover trademark records kept by the U.S. Patent and Trademark Office (USPTO). If your name is not found there, you can add another dip by having your attorney search trademark records kept by the individual states. There is even a triple dip option – a search of the Yellow Pages and the Internet to determine whether your name is being used in the broader marketplace. Of course, you may prefer – or have need for – a giant waffle cone. In that case, your attorney may recommend engaging a search service to conduct the most thorough search currently available, and that may include searching registrations and usage in foreign countries. After the search firm has submitted a report, your attorney is likely to prepare a legal opinion for you. The opinion will indicate any limitations on the use of your business name, geographic areas where a trademark owner has a right to prevent you from using your business name, and the extent to which you can protect your trademark.

If the search suggests that no other business is using your name or a similar name, the attorney then can file with the USPTO for a trademark registration. If the search reveals that your name or a similar name is already registered, you still may be able to register your name, but registration will be more difficult. Before proceeding your attorney may suggest that you investigate whether the registered owner is actively using the trademark. If the trademark is not in use or if the commercial use by its registered owners is substantially different from yours, you may want to approach the owner for an assignment or license of the registered trademark. The question, of course, is will they accept your price once they learn you have something of value?

If all else fails, you may simply have to change your name. It's natural that business owners develop an attachment to the name of their business and that changing it can be an emotionally charged process. But a name change is basically like any other change an owner must make from time to time, and in franchising the long-term benefits of choosing a protectable name for your business far outweigh the costs – financial or emotional – of making the change. Besides, if your existing name is not capable of receiving a trademark, it is fairly certain that your business operation, not the name, has been responsible for your success. A new name and distinctive logo may enhance both your existing business and the chances of rapid growth for your franchise.

The Franchise Agreement

Once the tasks of forming a corporation and obtaining a federal trademark registration have been addressed, your franchise attorney will begin the process of drafting a Franchise Agreement. In general, the purpose of the Franchise Agreement is to assure that:

1. Both parties have a clear understanding of their roles in the operation of the franchise.

2. The arrangement is fair for both parties.

3. Uniformity throughout the franchise system is established and preserved.

4. Standards of operations are prescribed.

5. Both parties are protected.

6. Future problems are anticipated and deviations discouraged.

7. Remedies for potential difficulties are provided.

You will be glad that you and your franchise attorney

have considered all of the issues discussed in Chapter 6. She or he will ask for your preferences on the type of franchise desired, franchisee training and support, franchise fees, royalties, advertising fees, etc. so that they can be articulated in your Franchise Agreement. By the way, before choosing a franchise attorney you may want to ask for a list of the topics to be covered in that agreement. Then, compare that list with the following outline. If it measures up well, you can be fairly confident in your choice of attorney. If not, go somewhere else.

The Franchise Agreement
Topic Outline

A federal law and the laws of many states require that every franchise company submit to its prospective franchisees a document that specifies in detail the terms under which franchisor and franchisee will work together. Perhaps no one part of the franchise development process is as important to the ultimate success of the franchise as the drafting of the contract between franchisor and franchisee, commonly known as the Franchise Agreement.

A good Franchise Agreement not only incorporates all of the elements of a sound business contract, it expresses in legal terms business decisions vital to the proper operation of the franchise. The following checklist of topics is derived from the examination by Francorp legal consultants of hundreds of Franchise Agreements and the drafting of hundreds of others. It can be used both as a guide to business decisions every new franchise company must make and as a format for the

Franchise Agreement itself.

1. Grant and franchise fee

2. Location/territorial rights
    a. Right to approve sites
    b. Right to prime lease
    c. Right to approval of lease
    d. Right to require inclusion of specific lease terms
    e. Tie the lease term to the Franchise Agreement term
    f. Plans and specifications
    g. Equipment must conform to specifications
    h. Determine territory
    i. Reserve right to distribute products through other distribution channels

3. Proprietary marks
    a. Use of name – rights, requirements and limitations
    b. Contest of name
    c. Notification to franchisor of other's use of name
    d. Reserve right to change the name
    e. Conformance to Operations Manual
    f. Use products, systems and supplies as specified
    g. Sign requirements

4. Training and assistance
    a. Must successfully complete training
    b. Start-up assistance

5. Franchisor's on-going operations assistance
   a. Continuing advisory service
   b. Promotional materials and bulletins, marketing
   c. Developments, products and techniques

6. Advertising
   a. Approval of all advertising copy, materials, packaging and promotional materials
   b. Establishment of national advertising fund
   c. Local advertising
   d. Co-op advertising
   e. Grand opening advertising requirements
   f. Limitations on Internet advertising

7. Operations Manual
   a. Must adhere
   b. Confidential
   c. Property of franchisor
   d. Cannot modify basic terms of Franchise Agreement

8. Confidential information
   a. Know-how, techniques and product formulas are trade secrets
   b. Protection necessary

9. Maintenance and repairs
   a. Maintain interior and exterior
   b. Create fund for refurbishing

10. Accounting and records
    a. Must keep complete records as prescribed
    b. Provide for reports
    c. Allow for inspection and copying of records
    d. Provide for audited statements
    e. Weekly reports and payments of royalty
    f. Access to franchisee's point-of-sale computer system

11. Standards of quality and performance
    a. Establish need for uniformity
    b. Provide for purchases which conform to specifications
    c. Dictate type, quality and quantity of purchases
    d. Specify when agreement commences
    e. Determine hours and days of operation short of agency relationship
    f. Require best efforts
    g. Reserve right to satisfy a customer's complaint at franchisee's expense
    h. Allow for inspection of quality and performance
    i. Reserve right to designate approved suppliers

12. Modification of system
    a. Establish right of franchisor to modify
    b. Prohibit franchisee from unauthorized modification

13. Continuing services and royalty fee
    a. Establish royalty
        1) Determine program necessary to provide ongoing support and consulting service
        2) Project total direct and indirect costs of providing continuing services
        3) Establish percentage of royalty and continuing service fee to provide for use of franchisor's name, concept and system
        4) Ensure payment of royalties

14. Insurance
    a. Protection for franchisee and franchisor
    b. Establish amounts of protection necessary
        1) Worker's compensation
        2) General liability-products-bodily injury
        3) Property damage
        4) Industry requirements

15. Term and renewal
    a. Determine term
        1) Renewal and termination provisions must comply with laws
        2) Renewal conditioned on updating image of facility
        3) Coordinate with lease
        4) Long term
            • Ensures royalty longer to franchisor
            • More security for franchisee

5) Short Term
- Adjust royalty upward if desired
- Eliminate undesirable franchisees
- Allows for earlier execution of new terms and conditions

6) Covenants
- During term and after termination
- Establish restrictions of franchisee's ability to compete, divert business, hire away employees and divulge secrets-subject to state and antitrust laws
- Franchisor's remedies

16. Termination and defaults
   a. Notice to cure – varies from state to state
   b. Bankruptcy
   c. Failure to select site, develop or open
   d. Failure to successfully complete training program
   e. Failure to pay royalties or fees
   f. Failure to submit reports or financial data
   g. Vacation or abandonment of premises
   h. Unapproved relocation
   i. Unapproved sale of franchised business
   j. Failure to comply with Franchise Agreement
   k. Failure to comply with Operations Manual
   l. Injury to system and marks
   m. Loss of license
   n. Other causes established by law

17. Rights following default
    a. Franchisor's right to operate
    b. Franchisor's right to discontinue selling products or services to franchisee

18. Rights and duties of parties upon expiration or termination
    a. Franchisee must pay all sums owing
    b. Franchisee must cease using name
    c. Franchisor's right to purchase physical assets
    d. Franchisor's right to signage and items identified by marks

19. Transferability of interest
    a. Provide conditions under which franchisee can sell
       1) Transfer fee
       2) Right of approval
       3) Payment of fees and sums
       4) Not unreasonably withheld
       5) Require new franchisees to complete training
       6) Require new franchisee to sign Franchise Agreement
       7) Require general releases if permitted by state law
       8) Right to require modifications and/or refurbishment

20. Death of franchisee
    a. Survivors can apply to continue
    b. Survivors can sell
    c. Franchisor can buy assets and real estate
    d. Provide formula for buy-out

21. Right of first refusal
    a. Franchisee must notify franchisor of bona fide offer
    b. Franchisor can buy at same price as buyer

22. Operation in event of disability or death
    a. Franchisor's right to operate
    b. Hold harmless

23. Taxes and permits
    a. Require payment of taxes, assessments, liens, equipment and previous accounts
    b. Require compliance with all federal, state and local laws
    c. Require obtaining of all permits, certificates and licenses necessary

24. Relationship
    a. Not agent, partner, or employee of franchisor
    b. Cannot incur liability to franchisor
    c. Franchisee bears cost of defense of claims
    d. Require conspicuous "Independent Franchise Owner/Operator" notice

25. Non-waiver
    a. Non-enforcement by franchisor is not a waiver
    b. Receipt of payments not a waiver

26. Notice
    a. Manner of notice
    b. Date of notice

27. Liability for breach enforcement
    a. Payment of costs and attorney's fees by party in default

28. Entire agreement
    a. Overrides any previous agreements
    b. Provides for amendments, changes or variance only if in writing

29. Severability
    a. Each section of Franchise Agreement is severable
    b. Franchisor can terminate Franchise Agreement if parts found illegal affect basic consideration of Franchise Agreement

30. Applicable law
    a. Specify which state's laws apply
    b. Subject to requirements of state law

31. Dispute resolution (where and when applicable)
    a. Arbitration
       1) Provides for selection of arbitrators
       2) Binding arbitration
    b. Mediation

32. Franchisee acknowledges receipt of FTC or UFDD documents

33. Franchisee
    a. Define term "franchisee" to include successors

34. Caveat
    a. Disclaimer as to claims made
    b. Franchisee assumes risks
    c. Success of business cannot be guaranteed
    d. Success of business depends on
       franchisee's ability
    e. Disclaimer re: FTC rule and disclosure

If all this detail seems excessive, we can assure you that the first time a question arises and you thumb through the Franchise Agreement to see whether or not the subject has been addressed, you will be delighted to find that it has. In fact, one of the purposes of the Franchise Agreement not listed above is to anticipate problems that might occur between the franchisor and the franchisee. Specific treatment in the Franchise Agreement of topics in this or a similar outline is your best guarantee of no surprises when difficulties arise.

Your franchise attorney will submit the completed Franchise Agreement to your local attorney.

The Franchise Disclosure Document

In Chapter 6 we mentioned that in the 1970s some states and later the federal government regulated franchising. That regulation primarily mandated the use of Offering Circulars. Offering Circulars have long been required for public companies. They inform investors about the companies and their officers, thereby minimizing the opportunity for fraud by unscrupulous sellers of securities. Offering Circulars of franchisors played precisely the same role. After the rule was passed, franchisors were required to create a Uniform Franchise Offering Circular (UFOC) and distribute that document to the prospective franchisee in every state at the time a sales presentation was made. More recently, in July 2007, the Federal Trade Commission (FTC) changed the name of the document to Uniform Franchise Disclosure Document (UFDD) and made minor changes to the rule itself. To obtain information for the Disclosure Document, your franchise attorney will submit a questionnaire.

Some of the principal topics include:

- The nature of the franchise and its market.
- Predecessor or parent companies or affiliates, if any.
- Biographies of the director, principal officers, other executives and franchise brokers or sales agents. In addition to information given in ordinary resumes, the biographies must reveal any convictions for felonies or misdemeanors, violations of franchise or related laws such as whether the person has filed for bankruptcy.
- Additional fees charged and the purpose of those fees.
- Whether some products or services must be purchased or leased by the franchisee from the franchisor and what percentage of the initial investment and ongoing expenses such purchases entail.
- Rebates, commissions, or other considerations the franchisor will receive from suppliers.

- What, if any, electronic cash register or computer systems the franchisee must buy or use.
- Information about franchisee training
- Listing of any trademarks, patents or copy-rights owned by the franchisor.
- Names of any existing franchisees and plans for selling franchises in the coming year.

The UFDD will also include a copy of your financial statement and any declaration of earnings that you care to make. From a legal standpoint, the UFDD is probably your most important document. In fact, the franchise agreement becomes part of the UFDD.

State registrations and filings

There is a third part to the legal process of becoming a franchisor. If you plan to sell franchises in any of the twenty-three states listed below, you must either register or file with their governments. Although the nature of these registration and filing requirements varies widely from state to state, the bottom line is this: Your franchise attorney must send to most of them your articles of in-corporation, proof of trademark and your UFDD, which, of course, includes the Franchise Agreement. And, with the exception of Kentucky, you must pay them a fee.

The difference between registration and filing states is largely one of scrutiny. In filing states you will either send the documents themselves or certification that the documents exist, pay a fee, and that is that. In registration states, an examiner may look over your documents and request changes to comply with state laws. Some of these changes simply require rewording of documents. Others could be more stringent: a request, for example, to increase your liquid assets in order to assure the state that you will not be entirely dependent upon franchise fees for support of your initial franchisees. On the other hand, a few registration states do not require you to send in your documents at all if you have obtained a federal registration of your trademark.

If you are domiciled or incorporated in a state that requires registration, you must register there. Otherwise, whether or not you register or file in any of these states is a business decision. Some new franchisors who intend to sell franchises only in their home state for the first year or two do not register elsewhere at the beginning. However, if you plan a regional or national expansion within the next two years, it may be more advisable to register and file across the board in all twenty-three states that require it. The various states continually "raise the bar" on net worth or other requirements, and it's often best to get registered as soon as possible, before the conditions for registration become more onerous.

It should be noted that the federal government requires that you update the UFDD annually or whenever you make material changes to it. Some states also require that your registration be updated after a material change. As a result, you will probably need to retain your franchise attorney after the documents are prepared and registrations and filing take place.

Registration States	Registration Fees	Filing States	Initial Filing Fees
California	$ 675	Connecticut	$ 400
Hawaii	$ 125	Florida	$ 100
Illinois	$ 500	Kentucky	0
Indiana	$ 500	Maine	$ 25
Maryland	$ 500	Nebraska	$ 100
Michigan	$ 250	North Carolina	$ 250
Minnesota	$ 400	South Carolina	$ 100
New York	$ 750	Texas	$ 25
North Dakota	$ 250	Utah	$ 100
Rhode Island	$ 500		
South Dakota	$ 250	Total	$7,300*
Virginia	$ 500		
Washington	$ 600		
Wisconsin	$ 400		

* Some fees may change

The Operations Manual

It is not possible to enforce your operational standards unless you explicitly define them. And the more explicitly you define them the easier it is to enforce them. Therefore you need as a new franchisor to craft a detailed, easy-to-follow manual that the franchisee and his or her employees can use on a day-to-day basis, especially in the early days of the franchise.

Start by reviewing the entire operation of your business to determine what can and should be done exactly the same way by a franchisee. We find that sometimes our clients already have manuals of sorts describing various aspects of their operation. Much of this material, if you have it, can be incorporated in your franchise Operations Manual. But the new manual will need to provide much that is in your head but not on paper, such as how to hire and train employees, do payroll, negotiate a lease, obtain and negotiate with suppliers, apply for sales tax ID numbers, OSHA requirements and myriad management functions. In addition, issues of gender, race, religion, and age discrimination need to be addressed and policies documented. Whenever Francorp writes an Operations Manual our Legal Department reviews it thoroughly to be certain that legal issues are addressed. You may at some time need to defend or enforce your operational standards in a court of law and you need to be sure you are on solid ground. The Operations Manual is also one of your most important and effective training tools. You will use it in whole to train a franchisee or in part for training employees. It is also a valuable selling tool. If your Operations Manual is complete and comprehensive, prospective buyers will be impressed. It will also help to allay their fears regarding how difficult it may be to learn the business.

Following are two examples of outlines for Operations Manuals, one for a service business, the other for a restaurant business:

FRANCHISE OPERATIONS MANUAL
Preliminary Outline

SERVICE BUSINESS

i. Title/Copyright Page

ii. The Franchise Operations Manual
A description of how the manual should be used and how it will be updated

iii. Statement of Confidentiality
> *A one-page statement of the franchisee's responsibility to keep the manual confidential; to be signed and returned by the franchisee*

iv. Notice of Policy/Procedure Change
> *The form used to notify the franchisee of a change in policy or procedure*

v. Submitting Suggestions to the Franchisor
> *Instructions for using a form to submit suggestions to the franchisor*

vi. Limitations of This Manual
> *A disclaimer notifying the franchisee of the responsibility to know and comply with local laws and regulations applying to the business*

A. INTRODUCTION

Letter from the President
> *A one-page letter that welcomes the franchisee to the network*

History and Philosophy of the Franchisor
> *A one- to two-page discussion detailing when and why the business was founded, who founded it, how the public has accepted it, and where it is going*

Services of the Franchisor Organization
> *A discussion that briefly describes the services provided by the franchisor (e.g., training, advertising, operational consulting, enhanced purchasing power, etc.), as indicated in the Franchise Agreement*

Responsibilities of a Franchisee
> *A list of the responsibilities a franchisee must meet*

Visits from the Corporate Office
> *An explanation of how the franchisor will periodically monitor franchisee compliance with the system and assist the franchisee with operational issues, including a description of the role of the person who will be conducting the visits from the corporate office and the phone number*

Field Visit Confirmation Form
> *A sample form that will confirm that a field consultant has conducted a visit with a franchisee*

Franchise Survey Form
> *An objective and/or subjective form used to assess franchisee compliance with the standards of the franchisor*

B. ESTABLISHING A BUSINESS

Introduction

Your Status as an Independent Contractor
> *Taken from the Franchise Agreement, a reminder to franchisees that they are not agents of the franchisor and that they must disclose this to the public*

Setting Up Your Office

Maintaining Professionalism in Your Home
> *Guidelines for equipping and setting up a home office and effectively avoiding distractions*

Required Insurance Coverages
> *A list of the insurance coverages franchisees are required to obtain*

Required/Recommended Bank Accounts
> *A discussion on the types of accounts each franchisee should open (e.g., payroll, checking, savings, etc.)*

Leasing Office Space
> *A list of the specific lease provisions that are necessary to include in the lease before signing (if not a home office); based on provisions from Franchise Agreement*

Selecting the Right Phone Service
> *Guidelines for the appropriate telephone lines and services*

Special Licenses and Permits
> *A list of the types of licenses and permits that may be necessary to operate a franchise*

Required Equipment, Supplies, and Furnishings
> *A list of the required items (including specifications) that are needed to operate the franchise*

Vehicle Specifications
> *The specifications that must be met to standardize the business image*

Signage and Logo Specifications
> *The specifications that must be met to standardize the business image*

Recommended Initial Inventory (if service involves a product)
> *A listing of the recommended opening inventory to operate a franchise*

Paying Taxes
> *A discussion on the federal, state, and city taxes each franchisee will need to pay*

Paying Additional Fees
> *Descriptions of other fees a franchisee may incur during the franchise relationship; taken from the Disclosure Document*

The following topics apply to the franchisee as the business grows. They serve as guidelines for the franchisee in assessing staff needs, hiring practices, applicable labor laws, and job descriptions. The topics are optional and may be developed for the first draft or added at a later date.

Deciding to Hire Additional Staff
> *Criteria that help the franchisee analyze staffing needs*

Policy on Fair Employment Practices
> *A recital of equal employment opportunity law and its mandates for businesses*

Inappropriate Pre-Employment Inquiries
> *A list of the questions to avoid when interviewing applicants*

Wage and Labor Laws
> *A brief discussion about the federal laws governing wages and hours*

Complying with the Immigration Reform and Control Act of 1986
> *How to comply with the Act; includes sample of the I-9 form*

Policy on Sexual Harassment
> *Definition of sexual harassment and francisor's policy regarding it*

Job Descriptions
> *Job description for each staff position*

Protecting the Franchise System
> *A discussion addressing the advisability of having employees sign a non-disclosure and non-competition agreement*

The Non-Disclosure and Non-Competition Agreement
> *A sample agreement*

C. OFFICE PROCEDURES

Introduction

Suggested Office Hours
> *The recommended hours of operation (including holidays)*

Maintaining Customer Lists
> *Information on retaining data on old customers and adding information on new customers*

Scheduling Service Calls
> *Information on how to efficiently schedule customer work*

Keeping Work Logs
> *Guidelines on the use of work logs and the information to include in them*

Invoicing Customers
> *Procedures for sending invoices, including how often to send them*

Collections Procedures
> *How to effectively collect accounts receivable*

Receiving Payments
> *What procedures to follow when payment is received*

Banking Procedures
> *The general procedures to follow for banking, including how often to make bank deposits*

Franchise Reporting Requirements and Procedures
> *As required by the Franchise Agreement, the weekly, monthly, quarterly, and annual reports the franchisee must submit to the franchisor*

Statement of Gross Receipts
> *A sample of the form the franchisee completes and sends to the franchisor along with the royalty payment*

Advertising Activity Report
A sample of the form the franchisee completes and sends to the franchisor with the invoices to prove that the minimum required amount (as noted in the Franchise Agreement) has been spent on local advertising

Preparing Financial Statements
Introduction to the sample formats that follow

The Model Chart of Accounts

The Income Statement
A sample income statement format

The Balance Sheet
A sample balance sheet format

Customer Service
A description of the prescribed methods for properly and politely dealing with customers

Handling Customer Complaints
How to deal properly and effectively with customer complaints and concerns

Professional Knowledge
A discussion on the importance of being familiar with the service of the business to present accurate information to customers

Pricing Franchisee Services

Equipment Maintenance
> *Guidelines for preventive maintenance and the repair of equipment*

Ordering Equipment and Supplies
> *A discussion on how the franchisee is to use the sources approved by the franchisor*

List of Approved Suppliers
> *A list of all franchisor-approved suppliers, complete with names, addresses, and phone numbers*

Request to Change Supplier/Supply
> *A form used to notify the franchisor of a wish to change suppliers*

Ordering, Receiving, and Storing Procedures
> *Procedures including when, how much, and how often to order; includes how to check an order when it arrives and proper storage information*

D. SERVICE PROCEDURES

NOTE: The topics for this section need to be developed with input from the franchisor. What follows are suggested topic titles for discussion purposes.

Introduction

Preparing for Service Calls

Conducting Service Calls

Post-Service Call Procedures

E. SELLING FRANCHISEE SERVICES

Introduction

Identifying the Franchisee's Customers
   A listing of the types of customers who would desire this service

Prospect Identification
   Information on successful methods of providing potential customers with exposure to the concept; may include guidelines for Internet marketing, telemarketing, direct mail, direct sales, and other techniques

Prospect Management
   Methods for communicating with prospects and appropriate procedures for monitoring the contacts

Selling Franchisee Services to a Prospective Customer

The Franchisee's Advertising Program
>   *A discussion on the program's
>   components, including local and
>   system-wide advertising*

The Grand/Business Opening
>   *A reiteration of the required amount
>   of money to be expended on
>   Grand/Business Opening
>   advertising (as required in the Franchise
>   Agreement) and a discussion on
>   recommended opening activities*

Guidelines for Using Franchisor Marks
>   *How to properly display the trademarks*

Advertising Media
>   *The media forms recommended by the
>   franchisor (e.g., Yellow Pages, Internet,
>   newspapers and magazines, direct mail,
>   radio, television, specialty advertising,
>   publicity, etc.)*

Obtaining Approval for Advertising Concepts and
Materials
>   *The procedures for obtaining approval for
>   franchisee-developed advertising concepts
>   and materials*

Request for Advertising Approval
>   *The form to be used for requesting
>   approval of advertising materials from the
>   franchisor*

FRANCHISE OPERATIONS MANUAL
Preliminary Outline

RESTAURANT

i.   Title/Copyright Page

ii. The Franchise Operations Manual
> *A description of how the manual should be used and how it will be updated*

Statement of Confidentiality
> *A one-page statement of the franchisee's responsibility to keep the contents of the manual confidential; to be signed and returned by the franchise*

Notice of Policy/Procedure Change
> *The form used to notify the franchisee of a change in a policy or procedure*

Submitting Suggestions to the Franchisor
> *Instructions for using a form to submit suggestions to the franchisor*

Limitations of the Manual
> *A disclaimer notifying the franchisee of the responsibility to know and comply with local laws and regulations applying to the business*

A. INTRODUCTION

Letter from the President
> *A one-page letter that welcomes the franchisee to the network*

History and Philosophy of the Franchisor
> *A one- to two-page description detailing when and why the business was founded, who founded it, how the public has accepted it, and where it is going*

Services of the Franchisor Organization
> *A discussion that briefly describes the services provided by the franchisor (e.g., training, advertising, operations consulting, enhanced purchasing power, etc.), as indicated in the franchise agreement*

Responsibilities of a Franchisee
> *A list of the responsibilities a franchisee must meet*

Visits from the Corporate Office
> *An explanation of how the franchisor will periodically monitor franchisee compliance with the system and assist the franchisee with operational issues; includes a description of the role of the person who will be conducting visits from the corporate office and the phone number*

Field Visit Confirmation Form
> *A sample form that will confirm that a field consultant has conducted a visit with a franchisee*

Franchise Survey Form
> *An objective and/or subjective form used to assess franchisee compliance with the standards of the franchisor*

B. ESTABLISHING A BUSINESS

Introduction

Your Status as an Independent Contractor
> *A reminder to franchisees that they must disclose to the public that they are not agents of the franchisor; based on the provision in the franchise agreement*

Required/Recommended Bank Accounts
> *A discussion on the types of accounts each franchisee should open (e.g., payroll, general operating, savings, etc.)*

Selecting and Developing Your Site
> *An outline of the specific criteria franchisees should apply when selecting a site and the procedure to follow to secure approval of the site from the franchisor*

Required Lease Inclusions
> *A list of the specific lease provisions that must be included in the lease before signing; based on franchise agreement provisions*

Required Insurance Coverages
> *A list of the insurance coverages franchisees are required to obtain*

Special Licenses and Permits
> *A list of the types of special licenses and permits that may be necessary to operate a restaurant*

Contracting Utilities and Services
> *A list and brief description of the utilities and services necessary to operate a restaurant*

Decor Specifications
> *A list of the decor standards with which franchisees must comply to standardize the restaurant's look and image*

Signage and Logo Specifications
> *A list of specifications franchisees must meet to standardize the restaurant's signage*

Purchasing Foodservice Equipment and Supplies
> *A discussion about purchasing the equipment and supplies necessary to operate a restaurant, including equipment specifications and recommended small wares and expendables inventories*

Food Purchasing Specifications
> *A list of the required specifications for food purchases, including brand, quality, and quantity*

Recommended Initial Inventory
> *A listing of the recommended initial inventory needed to open a franchise*

Standards of Cleanliness
> *A discussion about the importance of maintaining standards of cleanliness, as well as a description of those standards*

Paying Taxes
> *A discussion on the federal, state, and county or town taxes each franchisee will incur*

Paying Additional Fees
> *Descriptions of other fees that may accrue during the franchise relationship; taken from the Disclosure Document*

C. MANAGING A RESTAURANT

Introduction

Scheduling Shifts
A discussion on how shifts are scheduled for a restaurant

Managing Inventory
A discussion on proper inventory handling procedures, including ordering, receiving, rotating, and storage

Using Approved Sources
An explanation of the requirement that a franchisee use only franchisor-approved sources for obtaining equipment and supplies for the restaurant

List of Approved Suppliers
A list of all franchisor-approved suppliers, complete with names, addresses, and phone numbers

Request to Change Supplier/Supply

Generating Profit
> *A discussion on the various ways a franchisee can actively work to generate revenue and build profits for the restaurant; topics may include:*
>
> *Increasing Sales*
> *Inventory Controls*
> *Labor Costs and Scheduling*
> *Cash Controls*
> *Portioning*
> *Small wares and Expendables Controls*
> *Maintenance Practices and Repairs*

Franchise Reporting Requirements and Procedures
> *As required by the franchise agreement, the weekly, monthly, quarterly, and annual reports the franchisee must submit to the franchisor*

Statement of Gross Receipts
> *A sample of the form the franchisee completes and sends to the franchisor along with the royalty payment*

Advertising Activity Report
> *A sample of the form the franchisee completes and sends to the franchisor with the invoices to prove that the minimum required amount (as noted in the Franchise Agreement) has been spent on local advertising*

Policy on Sexual Harassment
> *Definition of sexual harassment and franchisor's policy regarding it*

Profile of the Ideal Employee
> *A listing of the characteristics and background of a model employee*

The Recruitment and Selection Process
> *A full discussion on the recommended recruitment techniques (e.g., classified ads, present employee referrals, etc.) and the subsequent interviewing techniques for screening personnel*

Sample Classified Ad for Recruiting Personnel

Sample Application for Employment

Protecting the Franchise System
> *A discussion addressing the advisability of having employees sign a non-disclosure and non-competition agreement*

The Non-Disclosure and Non-Competition Agreement
> *A sample agreement*

The Trial Period
> *A description of the length of the new employee's probationary period and how this period should be handled*

Work Opportunity Tax Credit
> *A discussion about the federal tax credit available to employers who hire workers from select groups (e.g., economically disadvantaged youths, veterans, handicapped, etc.)*

Establishing Personnel Policies
> *A discussion on the importance of setting personnel policies*

Personnel Policy Worksheet
> *A worksheet of topics that assists franchisees in developing personnel policies of their own*

Job Descriptions
> *Job descriptions for each position in the restaurant*

Employee Orientation and Training
> *General guidelines in this area*

Scheduling Employee Work Hours
> *Guidelines for effectively staffing a restaurant*

Time Reporting Procedures
> *Recommended procedures for recording an employee's hours*

The Uniform/Dress Code
>   *A description of the specific dress requirements for employees*

Evaluating Employees
>   *A discussion detailing how to conduct employee evaluations, how often they should be done, and the records that should be kept*

Discipline and Termination
>   *Appropriate techniques to follow when disciplining and/or terminating an employee, and any forms that should accompany these actions*

E. DAILY PROCEDURES

Introduction

Suggested Restaurant Hours
>   *The recommended hours of operation (including holidays)*

Daily Opening and Closing Duties
>   *A list of opening and closing procedures*

Time Reporting Procedures
>   *Recommended procedures for recording an employee's hours*

Preparing the Bank Deposit
> *A description of the procedure for making bank deposits for the business*

Food Preparation Procedures (optional)
> *The recipes and preparation procedures for each menu item*

Recipes (optional)

"To Go" Orders
> *A description of recommended carryout procedures*

Catering
> *A description of recommended catering policies and procedures*

Delivery (if applicable)
> *A description of recommended delivery procedures*

Responsible Beverage Sales
> *General information regarding the sale and service of alcoholic beverages*

Safety Concerns
> *A discussion on recommended procedures to avoid accidents*

F. ADVERTISING

The Advertising Program
> *A description of the advertising program, including advertising requirements*

The Value of Advertising
> *A general advertising philosophy*

Guidelines for Using Franchisor's Marks
> A list of guidelines to be applied when using marks

The Grand Opening
> A reiteration of the required amount of money to be expended on Grand Opening activities, as required in the Franchise Agreement, and a discussion on how the franchisee should go about planning and conducting Grand Opening activities

Advertising Media
> *The media forms recommended by franchisor (e.g., Yellow Pages, Internet, newspapers and magazines, direct mail, radio, television, specialty advertising, publicity, etc.)*

Sample Ads
> *Examples of ads*

Obtaining Approval for Advertising Concepts and Materials
The procedures for obtaining approval for franchisee-developed advertising concepts and materials

Ordering Advertising Materials from the Corporate Office
The procedures necessary to order ad slicks, scripts, etc.

If you are like most new franchisors you will have far better things to do than to write the Operations Manual yourself. The principal qualities needed in an Operations Manual writer are three: a familiarity with franchising, *including how franchise laws can impact a franchise program;* an understanding of how businesses work; and the ability to write in clear, concise English.

Chapter 9

Finding Your Franchise Prospects

We addressed in Chapter 6 the qualities a franchisee should have to be successful – willingness to follow the rules, work long hours, etc. But before you can be in a position to evaluate a franchise prospect sitting in the chair across from you five things have to happen.

1. You must establish in your mind a rough profile of your prospect.
2. You must identify where and how to find that candidate.
3. You must make contact with that person.
4. You must provide that person with information about your franchise.
5. You must "qualify" the prospect and persuade him or her to meet with you.

The first four of these activities fall under the category of franchise marketing. The fifth is the first step of the franchise sales process. In this chapter we'll discuss items one, two and three. Four and five will be dealt with in the chapters following.

Some franchisors begin the marketing process by defining their prospective franchisee in terms of professional qualifications, previous experience and financial resources. If your franchise is a conversion franchise, for example, your targeting can be extremely precise: real estate agents, optometrists, veterinarians, or whatever. If your business requires a low investment by someone who will do most of the work himself or herself, such as carpet cleaning, pet grooming, maid service, etc., you'll have a much wider market to address. But you'll also have a pretty clear picture of the kind of person you're looking for.

The vast majority of new franchisors will have less defined targets. They will attempt to reach the huge group of people who simply want to own their own business. That group has changed over the years. In the early days of contemporary franchising, the Fifties and Sixties, most buyers of franchises were "moms and pops" – the schoolteacher, the truck driver, the person with $25,000 who would be happy with an annual income of $30,000 per year. They were the backbone of franchising and many became wealthy as franchising grew. People like them are still buying the less expensive franchises referred to above, but in the past two decades a whole new breed of franchise buyers has emerged.

Among prime franchise prospects today are displaced corporate personnel, many of whom are victims of layoffs, mergers or bankruptcies. There are change-of-lifers, divorcees and retirees, young singles, couples, minorities, and women. Many of these people are un-sure of which particular franchise they want to buy, or even what industry they are interested in. They simply want to buy a franchise. The perception of the public, thanks to McDonald's, Holiday Inn, Midas, Terminex, Service Master, et al, is that a franchise is a good busi-ness, period! Any franchise! Of course, that mindset, to the extent that it exists, benefits all franchisors.

Having more or less established a profile for your prospective franchisees, the next step is to find them – in the most economical way possible. Toward that end every new franchisor should have a Marketing Plan. A proper Marketing Plan designed for the first year of the franchise program will answer questions such as:

- What should be our first year goal in franchise sales?
- How much should we spend to obtain those sales?
- What markets shall we move into and how quickly?
- What type of publicity can we generate? Who will do it?
- What advertising media, if any, shall we use: Search engine marketing (Internet), print, broadcast, direct mail, or all of the above?
- If we use the Internet, what search engines should we choose? How do we go about it?
- Should we attend franchise or trade shows? How many and where?
- Will we need a franchising specialist or consultant to help with marketing?

There's another question that the marketing plan should address: How best can we use our web site, or if we don't have one how do we create one? But because that topic fits under the heading of "telling your story," we'll deal with it in the next chapter.

Let's address these questions one by one.

The goal and budget

First, your franchise sales goal. That will depend to some extent on the size and cost of your franchise and the size of your budget. But for a franchise of average size (say a $300,000 total investment) you might conservatively set as your goal for the first year eight to ten franchise sales. (If the investment required is less than $100,000 the goal could be considerably higher.) Next, decide how much you're willing to pay for each sale. In order to "prime the pump," so to speak, you might want to spend a larger percentage of your total franchising budget for generating leads at the beginning than you will later on. If your franchise fee is $35,000, for example, you might decide to spend $7,000 or $8,000 for each of the ten franchises you expect to sell. That gives you a total of $70,000 to $80,000 for lead generation in the first year. Now you have your goal and you have your ad budget.

Initial market

Most new franchisors are well advised to start looking for franchisees close to home. That means within no more than two hours drive time from your headquarters. Getting on an airplane every time you want to service a franchisee is normally not the best way to start a franchise. Targeting your initial franchise sales activity in your immediate area keeps other costs down as well. Prospect meetings, follow-up meetings, sales closings, training, site assistance and startup assistance can be expensive for franchisor and franchisee alike when distances are involved. Besides, many companies find that the first few sales are made to existing customers. Once the word gets out that you are going to franchise, you may be surprised at how many people come forward without having to advertise for them.

Publicity

With that in mind, it's important to obtain all the free publicity you can. A press release announcing your decision to franchise should be sent to newspapers, radio stations and TV stations in your market area. That release and another designed for newly opened franchises should be included in your Marketing Plan. In addition, you'd be surprised how much "press" you can generate personally by calling business editors of your local papers and news editors of your radio and television stations to tell them about your franchise program. You may not have given it much thought, but the media have a vested interest in the success of your franchise. Whether or not you advertise now, you'll almost surely do so as your franchise grows. Besides, becoming a franchisor – especially in small and medium-size markets – has genuine news value. Expect to be interviewed and have your facilities photographed and videotaped.

Search engine marketing—a new world

In the world of franchising nothing has changed in the past decade as much as the way franchisors find new franchisees. In the 1990s about 16 percent of the people who indicated an interest in owning a franchise (what we call "leads") were referred by other people. That hasn't changed. In the Nineties about 12 percent were customers of the franchisor's business. That hasn't changed. But whereas in the Nineties the remaining 72 percent of leads came from print advertising or direct mail, today, according to Franchise Update Magazine, only 2 percent of all franchise leads comes from that source! The remaining 70 percent comes from the Internet, which, of course, did not exist as a viable advertising medium before 1995.

This figure may be somewhat distorted in favor of the Internet and to the disadvantage of print media for the following reason: even ads for franchises in the print media usually list a telephone number and a website. Many prospects go first to the franchisor's website to get a better idea of what the franchise opportunity consists of before making actual contact with the franchisor. And then, instead of using the phone, they indicate their interest on line. Thus, the franchisor may never know that the original source of the lead is a publication, not the Internet.

But distortion or not, the Internet has had an undeniably profound effect upon franchise marketing – as it indeed has had on commerce of all kinds. Think about it for a moment. In 1990 the primary way people learned about a franchise opportunity was to 1) visit the place of business; 2) meet a representative at a trade show or other event; or 3) obtain a copy of the franchise brochure. Today, anyone in the world can type a few letters on a screen, access a website and obtain whatever information the franchisor is willing to give. That is why today nothing is more important to franchise marketing than having a website. Actually, more than nine out of ten business owners we talk to do have a website. We'll discuss what to do if you don't and how to make your existing website franchise friendly in the next chapter. In the meantime, let's address the matter of how your Marketing Plan can help you obtain leads through the Internet and elsewhere.

Speaking of free publicity, you can get it on the Internet, too – if you have a website. To illustrate, if you have a computer nearby, go to your favorite search engine – Google, MSN, Yahoo, etc. – and type in a one or two-word description of your franchise. For example, suppose you go to Google and type in "pizza franchise." Your screen will be divided into three parts. At the top will be two or three listings with yellow background. At the right in column form will be several other listings. And below and to the left of these listings will be other listings related to pizza franchises. The listings at the top and at the right are paid for. We'll talk about those later. But the listings that dominate the page are called "organic." That means that these listings are generated by Google's search of websites on a more or less random basis. ("More or less" because whatever criteria Google uses for such searches are not disclosed and are subject to change anyway.) So if you are a pizza franchisor and if you have a website that is correctly structured you have a chance of appearing on Google's page one (or on succeeding pages) for "pizza franchise" at no cost whatever. Another reason to get a website if you don't have one.

Structuring a website so that it will have the best chance of appearing organically on search engines is one form of Search Engine Marketing. The other is Pay-per-Click (PPC). To return to the example given above: Owners of the paid-for listings are paying Google every time someone clicks on their website. Because you pay only to give your message to people who express an interest, PPC advertising is highly favored for big ticket advertisers like franchisors, who are targeting a very small number of people in a very large marketplace. And what makes PPC advertising even more attractive is that it can be precisely targeted geographically. If you're planning to limit your franchise market to, say, Paducah, KY, you can use PPC advertising to target only zip codes within and adjacent to that city if you wish. Of course, you may have to pay a premium to get one of the top listings in the markets you choose, but it could be worth it.

One more thing about Search Engine Marketing. You'll want to be careful about selecting the key words that people type to bring up your listing. For example, if you're a pizza franchisor, you may not want to limit your market to people who type in "pizza franchise." You may want to broaden it to people who simply type in "franchise" or "franchises for sale." That widens your net and also costs more. Another thing: the more specific the words used, the more likely that the consumer will find what she or he is looking for. And in your case, the more likely you'll find a qualified prospect. Another problem is selecting search engines. At this writing there are seven in all. Which should you choose? Because search engine marketing is so new and so specialized you may find it useful to get qualified assistance.

By the way, you'll find if you go on the Web and look under "franchises for sale" or "franchises" that the companies listed in the prime time spots at the top are rarely franchise companies. Usually they are websites of companies that allow prospects to select from a variety of franchisors in various types of businesses. Franchisegator.com is one. So is FrancorpConnect.com. Companies like these pay substantial amounts to be listed at the top of the page on search engines like Google in all geographic areas. They also advertise heavily in trade journals and on the Internet. (Francorp takes part in franchise shows and trade shows and conducts more than 150 seminars each year to generate leads for its clients who are listed on FrancorpConnect.com.) To be listed with such companies you'll pay either a reasonable monthly fee or a price per lead. When a prospect scrolls through the franchises listed at one of these sites and wants to know more about yours, he or she will be asked to provide personal information including available cash, type of business preferred, where they want to locate their business, educational background and work experience. At FrancorpConnect.com prospects can also take a test to help them determine whether or not have the qualities needed to be a franchisee. If they spend more than a few minutes on your listing, their application and test are automatically emailed to you.

If they're in a hurry, they can go directly to your company's website and ask to talk to a sales person.

As far as other media are concerned, television is generally too expensive for franchise marketing – especially for new franchisors – because small audiences cannot be targeted economically. Ditto for radio. Direct mail, unless you have a mailing list with special qualities (your own customers, for example) will probably not generate leads as well as the Internet. Your marketing plan should contain copy and layout for newspaper ads, however. Small ads, placed judiciously in business sections of the paper, can be effective.

Trade Shows

Trade shows offer franchisors the opportunity to combine Steps 1, 2, 3, 4 and even 5 mentioned early in this chapter. Prospective franchisees attend the shows, often paying an admission fee, and walk down the aisles stopping at booths that arouse their interest. The shows will charge an entrance fee and you must build, buy or rent a booth and have personnel available to speak to customers. When prospects appear, you will qualify them as to their degree of interest and financial capabilities, give them your printed material or let them watch a video, and make an appointment for a visit to your place of business. However, trade shows such as the International Franchise Exposition (IFE), held annually in cities like Washington, D.C., Los Angeles and Miami, where up to two hundred franchise companies congregate, are more likely to yield positive results to large, national franchises than to start ups. Of course, if a regional franchise show comes to a market you've targeted, attendance may be worth the expenditure. In addition, industry-specific trade shows can also be a source of franchise leads.

Getting help

As we noted, the principles of franchise marketing are much the same as those of marketing any other product or service. Even so, the price of a franchise coupled with the laws that relate to the sale of franchises (which we'll discuss later), mean that the process is necessarily more complex than selling an item in a store. It is even more complex than selling an automobile or, in some cases, a house. There is another factor that differentiates franchise marketing from most other marketing. In a real sense you will be awarding your franchises only to people who deserve them. As we have repeated throughout this book, the last thing you need, especially at the beginning, is a fast check from someone who is doomed to fail. So the entire process of franchise marketing and sales requires a certain discretion – forbearance if you will. Hard sell has no place in the franchise sales process. That is one reason for having people experienced in franchise marketing guide you in the early stages. It can save you a good deal of heartache – to say nothing of money – later on.

Chapter **10**

Telling Your Story

As a business offering franchises for the first time, you have a story to tell. How well you tell it in words and pictures will have a direct bearing on how speedily your franchise grows.

The story is about why your franchise differs from other franchises and why the prospective franchisee should regard it as a worthwhile investment. Be warned, however, that there is a difference between the stories you tell to sell your products and services and those you tell about your franchise. Exaggeration in everyday advertising is so common it's almost expected. But you have much less latitude for embellishment in advertising your franchise. Not that you can't use adjectives, but the facts that you present must be verifiable. If they're not and you seek to register your franchise in, say, California, the State may look at your advertising materials and say, "Sorry, you can't use them here."

If you've spent $5,000 printing a Franchise Brochure, making unverifiable claims could be a costly mistake.

The truth is, however, that there's no need to embellish. The right creative team – copywriter and designer – one sensitive to the need for accuracy, will know where to look to find the story that needs to be told. They will know how to present it in an enthusiastic, persuasive, imaginative way without distortion. That team will also be experienced in creating franchise marketing materials that are in compliance with federal and state requirements.

Your Franchise Brochure

The printed document that best tells your story will probably be your Franchise Brochure, typically eight pages long, 9 x 12 inches in size, and printed with color photographs. In addition, like many franchisors, you may want to include with the brochure a DVD that describes your business in even greater depth. In business, perception is everything. You will be competing with large franchise companies, so it's important that to the prospective franchisee your printed and visual materials present a thoroughly professional appearance. You don't have to be a Fortune 500 company to look like one.

A well-constructed Franchise Brochure differs from most other types of advertising because by its very nature it must tell two stories at the same time. It must, of course, explain to the franchise prospect why she or he will be making a good investment. But – and this is especially true of new franchisors – it must describe the business itself and show why it is attractive to custom-

ers. And the more distinctive your business the more comprehensive this description must be. For example, a franchise brochure created by Francorp's marketing department for Huffman Builders explained, of course, how the franchisee would use the Huffman system
to provide office condominiums for doctors, dentists, attorneys and other professional and business groups. But in addition the brochure described the thriving market for such condos by quoting sources such as The New York Times, National Real Estate Investor and Upsize Minnesota Magazine. Including statistics about the demands for your products and services is helpful in building credibility. And quoting your sources keeps regulators at bay.

Your brochure should do other things as well. It should tell something about the history of your business and how it became successful—focusing on the owners who prospects may be meeting later. It should point out the special advantages franchising offers franchisees. It should also describe the specific kinds of support your franchisee will receive, such as training, Operations Manual, marketing materials and on-site assistance at the Grand Opening and afterward. Finally, it should list the qualities and experience required of a franchise applicant and ask the reader to call for further information.

One more thing. Because the Franchise Brochure is an expensive document, it should be reserved for candidates you feel have at least a chance to qualify as franchisees. A less expensive Mini-Brochure can be created for handing out to casual browsers at trade shows.

Your Website

We hope we have demonstrated how important a website can be to your franchise program. To repeat, nothing has made as much difference to franchise marketing since the birth of McDonald's as the Internet. It is the elixir of franchising. It is advertising on steroids. And it's going to increase. While age demographics show increasing usage of computers and the Internet by people in their fifties and sixties, such use is explosive among thirty- and forty-year olds and at saturation in the teen through thirty-year olds. People over thirty are today's franchise buyers. Those under are the franchise buyers of tomorrow.

The odds are that you already have a website. If you do and you have decided to franchise, this is the time to re-evaluate it. Does it showcase your company in the best possible way? Does it allow visitors to find what they want quickly? Does it provide answers to their questions that are both clear and comprehensive? Many websites that provide plenty of places for the visitor to go offer very little information when they get there. That is probably because graphic designers traditionally have been in charge of creating websites. Be sure when you revise or add to your existing website or create a new one that you work with an experienced copywriter to tell your story in the best possible way.

If you do not have a website, now is the time to create one. As your business grows your website will almost certainly become indispensable in generating sales, even if you do not actually offer goods or services on the site. There are many ways to approach website design, including inexpensive ones that can be found on the Net. Two things to be aware of are these:

1. You will need a "domain name," the name that is used to identify your business on the Web. Ideally it will be the name of your business as it now exists, but if that name is taken it should be something as close to your name as possible. A domain name can be purchased on line with a credit card. And while you're at it, register any name that people might use because it's similar to yours. For example, if your name is stoneproductsinc.com you might also want to reserve stonesproductsinc.com and stoneproducts.com. If you haven't got a domain name, don't waste any more time. Get it now.

2. Make sure that your website is interactive. In other words, give the visitor the opportunity to respond on the Web. That is especially important for the franchise segment of your website. A prospect should be able to type in his name, address, and phone number – and perhaps other information as well – so that you can give an immediate reply. In the Age of the Internet, rapid response is critical.

Whether you are creating a new site or simply adding to an old one, the franchise portion should be separate from the rest of the site. Of course, it will be reachable by anyone who visits your home page. The words "Franchise Information" should be prominently displayed. But in addition, a visitor should be able to reach the franchise section directly by going to a search engine, typing in words that lead to your domain name (e.g. Stone Products) and adding the word "franchise." As for content, you will already have created a franchise brochure. Much of the franchise portion of your site can employ material from that brochure. Of course, the potential exists on the website for giving much more information than can be put into the brochure. The website can also contain more timely information, because websites can be updated much more easily. For example, as franchises are sold you can list their locations on your website and even include testimonials from franchisees. Favorable publicity can be copied to the site. And, depending upon your budget, you can even employ a short video presentation – a statement by the franchisor, for example – that can be downloaded by the prospect. By the way, the more material you have on your site, the greater the attraction it will have for search engines and the more likely that you'll be listed organically by them.

One caveat. To bulk up their sites some companies post their Disclosure Document, which includes the Franchise Agreement. We strongly recommend against this practice. The Disclosure Document is not a sales tool. It can intimidate the prospect and be a deal killer if introduced too early in the process. When you present this inch-thick document at the proper time, leafing through and explaining each section, you will take the mystery and complexity out of the equation. If, for some reason, you feel you must include the Disclosure Document on your website, be sure that only qualified applicants have access to it. You can do this by placing it in a protected area that can only be entered with a code you will give them.

Finally, before going on line with your website look at the websites of your competitors. Ask yourself how yours stacks up against theirs? If you need to go back to the drawing board, now is the time.

Follow-up

Once your brochure is printed and your website is working you are ready to respond to prospective franchisees. Actually, by that time you are already responding to franchisees. One reason the Internet has been such a boon to franchise sales is that the website is lead-generator and response mechanism all in one. In the "old days"– before 2000 – it was a different ball game. You placed an ad, waited for someone to call, sent out a brochure and waited again until it had been received, then made more calls, etc. – an exceedingly time consuming process. Now, when the prospect arrives at your website, whether guided there by a search engine or by a print ad, the prospect will have at hand enough information to make at least a preliminary decision as to level of interest. And if that person responds by giving you his or her email address, we recommend that you use an auto responder to send a return email thanking the person for the inquiry, offering additional information, and including an application. In the age of the Internet, when your prospect may be requesting information from several franchisors the one that responds the quickest and most efficiently will have a leg up.

In the best of all possible worlds the prospect will fill out the application you have sent and return it by email to you. You will examine the application to determine whether or not the prospect has the basic qualifications – financial and experience – to be a franchisee. If that person does, you or your sales staff will call to set up a meeting. Of course, in actuality the process may take somewhat longer. You may have several phone conversations before an application is sent. You may need to send your brochure, which includes an application. And surely some prospects will not qualify and others will lose interest. That is why it's critical to have a steady lead flow.

One more thing before we leave the lead generation process. A lead is not only a potential franchisee. It's a unit of measurement. The number of leads you receive, and especially the source of those leads, can tell you how well your franchise advertising dollars are being spent. If you buy PPC advertising in three search engines, for example, you can determine relatively quickly how they rank. Though these days it's more difficult to determine precisely the origin of the lead because print ads direct readers to websites, it's important that everyone who responds on line or elsewhere be asked how they first heard about you. Lead tracking is an important element of franchise marketing.

Chapter 11

Making The Sale

We have stated that the marketing and selling of franchises differs from the traditional marketing and selling you do as a business owner. For one thing, it usually requires making three sales simultaneously. You must first persuade the franchise buyer that a market exists for your products or services in the area they intend to locate. Sometimes that's relatively easy to do. Sometimes it requires considerable research. Second, you must convince the franchise buyer that specific aspects of your business make it a worthy investment. That sale is made easier to the extent that your business itself is distinctive or that certain qualities make it so. And thirdly, although it is becoming less and less necessary, you will sometimes have to sell franchising itself. After all, most of your prospects will never have owned a franchise. Many will need to be reminded of the virtues of franchising that we have discussed in earlier chapters.

In addition to the number of simultaneous sales you must make, there are two other differences between franchise and traditional selling. One has to do with the state and federal regulations. You must obey the rules or else. We'll discuss both the rules and or else in this chapter. The third difference has to do with the size of the sale. The average sale for most businesses is between $20 and $2000. In the franchise business an average sales is $150,000 to $200,000. It's simply not possible to sell a franchise in the same way you sell a chicken dinner or even an automobile. As a result of all of these differences you have two choices. One is to hire people experienced in franchise sales. The other is to obtain franchise sales training for you and any member of your company who will be involved in the franchise sales process. The trouble is that Choice #1 does not eliminate Choice #2. You need the training whether or not you hire experienced franchise sales people. We'll also discuss franchise sales training in this chapter.

There is yet one more difference between selling franchises and selling products or services that we have been emphasizing: in franchise sales selection of the franchisee is at least as important as making the sale. In Chapter 6 we discussed the qualities you should look for in a franchisee. Four in particular are critical.

1. Business experience. Without it, the franchisee may be unable to operate properly.
2. Capital. A franchisee who runs short of money may not survive the start-up period.

3. Willingness to work hard.* Disenchantment with long hours can be fatal.
4. Compatibility. The wrong person may resist taking your recommendations and following your suggestions.

But you may find that following the criteria we recommend during the selling process is not always as simple as it sounds. Difficulty can occur when a sales person, on commission, finds what appears to be a qualified individual who is ready to buy. The sales person introduces the candidate to you and during your interview you discover personal characteristics that you feel could prevent that person from being a successful franchise owner. You are now in the position of having to (1) disappoint the prospect and (2) disappoint the sales person. At the same time, you have a check for $25,000 or $35,000 or whatever the franchise fee happens to be sitting on the desk in front of you. In such a situation, we have no good way to console you – except to say that the penalty down the road for accepting the candidate can be far worse than the penalty for losing the sale. First, you may have an unsuccessful franchisee and thus a blight on your record that is visible to any new prospect. Second, you may eventually have a disgruntled franchisee eager to salvage some of his or her investment

---

* An article in the July 26, 2007 issue of *The New York Times* illustrated the importance of this point. It told about students who are leaving college early to buy franchises. One of them, 24-year-old Clay McGee, bought a 1-800-gotjunk franchise in Springfield, MO. Although in his third year the franchise cleared $120,000, by that time McGee had earned it. "I pictured myself having employees and playing golf, but I basically hauled junk for two years," he said, adding, "If you don't put in 90-hour work weeks, you're not going to succeed."

by suing you. So be firm. Do the right thing. Of course, you can avoid this type of situation by employing sales people who are properly trained. And you can prevent it during the early stages of your franchise program by being your own franchise sales person. If it is any consolation, you should know that 89 percent of the 229 franchisors who responded to a marketing and sales survey conducted by DePaul University and Francorp said they had turned down candidates who were financially qualified. Their principal reasons: personality/ attitude and unsuitable background.

Here are the basic steps to be followed in making a franchise sale:

- Use a lead sheet to keep track of inquiries.
- Devise (or obtain) a questionnaire to be used in qualifying prospects.
- If, during telephone conversations, the prospect appears to be qualified, arrange a face-to-face meeting.
- At the first such meeting deliver a Disclosure Document to the prospective franchisee.
- Arrange a meeting at your headquarters no earlier than ten days from the first meeting when the Franchise Agreement will be signed and you will receive a check from the candidate.

If this process seems simple, indeed it can be. But the new franchisor should be prepared for times when it is not. That is why as one of its services to clients subscribing to our full development program, our company provides a 482-page manual addressing the many nuances of franchise selling. The Francorp Franchise Sales Manual includes a comprehensive overview of the franchise sales process and detailed instruction in proven franchise sales techniques. Among other topics are proper lead follow-up procedures, state and federal legal requirements pertaining to franchise sales, presentations for franchise trade shows and sales seminars and much more. To give you an idea of the complexities involved in franchise selling, we are including an outline from that manual at the end of this chapter.

From a legal standpoint, the two most important aspects of the sales process listed above are delivery of the Disclosure Document and the ten-day waiting period. The FTC Rule requires both. Courts have awarded civil penalties of up to $11,000 for each violation of the Rule (as much as $870,00 in a single case) plus monetary redress on behalf of investors (as much as $4.9 million in a single case). In addition, courts have routinely granted preliminary freezes of both corporate and private assets in Rule violation cases. Similar penalties have also been given for earnings claims violations. As we have noted elsewhere, if you decide that you want to answer the question "How much can I make as a franchisee?" by showing sales and earnings of your own units or those of your franchisees you must do so by filing an earnings claim. If you do not file such a claim, neither you nor your sales person can answer that question. If you do, you are in violation of the FTC Rule. It is worth noting here that in the DePaul/Francorp survey only 15.9 percent of frachisors said that they used earnings claims, and that less than half of those that did use them regarded them as "very useful" in closing the sale.

Finally, if we were to recommend an initial "sales pitch" to a franchisee it would sound something like this:

"Buying a franchise is different from any purchase you have ever made. To begin with, it will probably be the most important purchase you've ever made. For most people it means not simply a change of career, but a change of lifestyle. In the past you worked for someone else. Now you will work for yourself. In the past you were an employee. Now you will be an employer. You will provide the capital to create the business. You will have full responsibility for it. As a result, when there are rewards you will be the first to benefit. And the harder you work, the more rewarded you are likely to be.

"But there is a second huge difference from any other purchase, and it is this. When you find an automobile or even a house for sale, the decision to buy once the price is agreed upon is yours and yours alone. If you buy our franchise, a second decision-maker will be involved: we, the franchisor. Franchising is a two-way street. You must want us, and we must want you. That is why we asked you to fill out a detailed application. We can only award you this franchise if we are convinced that you will succeed as a franchisee, just as you will only buy this franchise if you are convinced it will be a wise investment in every way.

"So let's proceed on that basis. You will learn about us. We will learn about you. And together, if everything goes well, we'll begin what we both believe will be a fruitful relationship. If not, we'll both have profited from the experience."

Francorp® FRANCHISE SALES STRATEGY™

EXHIBIT A

Table of Contents

SECTION 1: PROGRAM INTRODUCTION

SECTION 2: LEGAL ISSUES

SECTON 3: GETTING READY

SECTION 4: SALES PROCESS

SECTION 5: ADDITIONAL SALES METHODS

SECTION 6: CONCLUSION

SECTION 7: APPENDICES

Chapter 12

Following Through

At last, your franchise development program has been completed. Your strategic plan has been devised. Legal documents and operations manuals have been created. Marketing strategies and materials are in place. You are almost ready to sell your first franchise.

This is an excellent moment to step back and think about your forthcoming relationship with the people who will literally make or break your franchise program: your franchisees. First, let's examine your respective positions. You, as the franchisor, own the name and system. You will license to the franchisee the use of that name and system for an initial fee and an ongoing percentage of his or her sales. The franchisee may also become your customer, buying products or services from you. As the franchisor, you have the right, and more importantly the responsibility, to protect the name and system of your company. There can be no compromise of your standards, as you define them. The systems and procedures described in your Operations Manual must be followed exactly and explicitly with no deviations, unless, of course, you permit them. Your Franchise Agreement, if properly drafted, addresses this subject and identifies a formal procedure for a franchisee to request changes of procedures, products, services or systems. Again, you have the right and responsibility of enforcement.

Clearly the Franchise Agreement is a one-sided document. It has to be because you, the franchisor, bear the primary responsibility of protecting your name and system both on behalf of your corporation and on behalf of the franchisees themselves.

Your relationship with the franchisee is almost sure to change as the years go by. In the early stages it will resemble to some degree the relationship between parent and child. You will nurture, teach, train, and provide close supervision and support as you would an infant. The franchisee will hang on every word and look to you as a guru and do whatever you tell them to do without question. But just as children become adolescents and then adults, franchisees mature in their operation and management of their franchise. They deal with hundreds of customers, employees, and vendors. They mature in their operation and management of the franchise. Indeed, their views of current or proposed programs may in time differ from yours. At this point it can be fatal to the franchise to think of them or treat them as children. In fact, as expert witnesses we have testified too often in lawsuits between franchisors and franchisees that might never have been filed had the franchisors fully recognized the psychological differences between the company's new franchisees and the older ones.

So while you have the right and responsibility of enforcement, you need to balance these issues with the recognition that every franchisee is an independent owner of that business, *not* an employee. You cannot go into their place of business as though it were one of your offices or stores and order changes or address employees of that franchisee, as though they were your employees. Your communications must be advisory, collegial, motivational, constructive, and clear in your efforts to assist them in increasing sales and profits and making their operations more effective in *their* best interests. Remember, the more successful they are, the more successful *you* will be. Successful and happy franchisees are your best franchise salespeople.

When we talk about support, we refer to a meaningful, regular, and consistent dialogue with your franchisee. We recommend a one- to two-month training period for the franchisee and perhaps one or two of the franchisee's key employees at your headquarters, followed by a one- to two-week visit by your representative at their place of business to help hire and train your franchisee's employees. Simply training your franchisees and allowing them to go off and open their units is not enough. Even franchisors with thousands of units agree that no two units operate exactly the same. For one thing, the customer base differs from market to market and even from unit to unit in the same market. A new franchisee lacks the experience to read the subtleties of equipment, product, service, and customer differences, as well as other nuances in their new businesses, and will need your expertise to make whatever adjustments are appropriate. No matter how extensive and intensive the initial training program at your headquarters training facility, once they get to their own site and the doors open, they will be in shock and will need your hand holding until they get on track.

Once they are open, we recommend the following field support visitation schedule:

Once a week for the first quarter
Every other week for the second quarter
Every third week for the third quarter
Once a month thereafter

These visitations will be as "consultants," *not* the "Gestapo." We strongly oppose "secret shopper" or unannounced "check-up" visits. Pejorative visits like these only alienate franchisees. Remember, you are there to help, not to find fault. You should make an appointment for the visit, announce its purpose, and suggest an agenda to the franchisee in advance. "Hi, John, this is Pat. I'd like to come out to your unit next week. Would Thursday be okay? I noticed in your P & Ls that your labor costs have been creeping up. Maybe we can sit down and go over them and maybe I can help you get a handle on this." Or: "We have a new product line that will be coming out in the spring, and I'd like to go over it with you and your staff." These are positive and constructive approaches toward developing and maintaining good relations with your franchisees. While monitoring operations is critical to ensure quality control, you must understand that your main role is to provide *leadership* and *direction*. You should be the

Number 1 cheerleader. Remember, your franchisees are collaborators not underlings.

Of course, if you make the mistake of selling a franchise to the wrong person, you can expect a number of problems, including a lack of adherence to your program and procedures; sloppy execution; substitution or addition of non-approved products, services or unauthorized ingredients; understaffing; lack of maintenance; late payment of royalties; disputes with vendors; or many irritating issues which, while not reaching the level to justify termination, will drive you crazy, nonetheless. This is why we place so much emphasis on *selection, selection, selection* of the right franchisee.

It is particularly important to respond and act immediately when any deviation or lack of compliance occurs. Don't let it go, especially early on, because you set the stage for bigger problems and more of them. Deal with these issues early on in a congenial, supportive, motivational manner. Always document *every* phone call, visit, discussion, and, especially, deficiency. When making your weekly and monthly visitations, always prepare a visitation report before you leave and give a copy to the franchisee, documenting the issues discussed and have them sign it. If the occasion ever does arise when you must take action to terminate them, you will need documentation to show a pattern of non-compliance.

As a franchisor, you must also balance the goal of saturating a market in order to have full representation with the concern of not wanting to encroach on an existing franchisee's customer base. Encroachment has been one of the most frequently litigated issues of franchisor/franchisee disputes. You may be on safe legal ground in placing a unit in an area, but by doing so you may create a serious breach of a good relationship with an existing franchisee. This issue is further complicated by the fact that demographics change. Where one of your units needed a population base of 50,000 to be successful, the addition of new products, services, and a greater acceptance of your concept may change those demographics to needing only 25,000 people to be successful.

On the one hand, our goal is *market saturation*, not just *market penetration*, and we need to protect ourselves from competitors who will move into the market. On the other hand, franchisees will understandably be upset by the addition of another franchise in what they perceived to be their market, even though their Franchise Agreement limited the area of their market or provided, as we recommend, no exclusive territory. McDonald's, which gives no exclusive territory or protected radius, does, however, compensate a franchisee if a new unit is located in an adjacent area, and it affects the original franchise's sales by more than 10 percent. McDonald's also has an Ombudsman program to resolve disputes internally and avoid, if possible, arbitration, mediation or litigation.

Another area of sensitivity is the Advertising Fund. Most franchisors require that franchisees contribute to a fund to be used for local, regional or national advertising. These funds are collected by you, the franchisor, and kept in a separate account. The only expenditures allowed from that account are for the actual ad costs, creative work, Internet advertising, and staff costs directly relating to consumer advertising or any expenses that are attributable to it. It is extremely important for you to understand that these are not your funds. They are the franchisees' funds, and you are responsible for the appropriate disbursement and care of these funds. While there has been litigation on whether or not you have a "fiduciary" responsibility, you should be extremely careful to be sure that these funds are appropriately handled and expended. We recommend that you provide franchisees with a quarterly report on the use of these funds. The Advertising Fund has often been a subject of litigation and dispute between franchisors and franchisees.

As noted earlier, we recommend forming a Franchisee Advertising Council, composed of representative franchisees from each market, usually no more than ten. Provide them with proposed advertising program ideas and solicit their input. This council will be advisory, and while you are not legally obligated to accept their recommendations, you will usually receive excellent feedback and many good ideas relating to advertising. After all, they are the closest to line of fire from consumers. You would be well advised to listen.

While we're talking about councils, let's tackle the bigger council issue. We recommend forming a franchisee organization right from the beginning. It works much better if you help organize it, give it some form and agenda, and use it as a forum to guide their organization in a positive direction, focusing on common problems and interests. Help them form a board and elect officers. Develop an agenda that promotes the brand and the company, but allows for free expression, suggestions, new ideas, grievances, and a platform for featuring a different franchisee at each meeting with something they have done that has enhanced their operation and can be shared by the entire organization. Trust us – it is better to form this group initially, get them off on the right track, and then step out gracefully than to wait until, because of a lack of dialogue, they form a group out of frustration or disenchantment with you. These groups develop and maintain a spirit of camaraderie, an exchange of information, and can be a very positive force in the morale and success of your company. The downside is that it sometimes can be political or a platform for personal agendas. These can best be addressed by singling out the negative influences and trying, one on one, to work out their issues. You don't want to hear about a problem for the first time at the group meeting.

If you are doing your job, you will already be aware of any problems when you make your regular unit visitations and have open and non-confrontational dialogues with your franchisees. Once again our advice: do everything you can to make your franchise owners happy and successful. It is in your best interest as well as theirs!

Although the theme of this book is franchise development, we have been addressing in this chapter two topics that become relevant only after the development program has been completed: franchisor/franchisee relations and franchisor/franchisee marketing. We have done so simply because we believe that the attitude you take toward your franchisees and the programs you put in place on their behalf will be critical to the success of your franchise program. However, there are other issues you will need to address while your franchise development program is underway or soon afterward. To cover these issues, which include franchisor/franchisee relations, Francorp offers its clients a management training program. Some of the questions this program addresses are: How do you establish an organization that will simultaneously run your franchise program and operate your core business? How many people will you need, what skills should they have and at what point should you bring them on board? What will your training program consist of, how long will it last, and who will be responsible? What will your field support program provide and who will do it? What does franchisor compliance mean and how do you respond?

The following is a topic outline for that program:

FRANCORP ®
FRANCHISE MANAGEMENT TRAINING
Franchise University™
Training Agenda

INTRODUCTION
- Objectives of the Franchise Management Training Program
- Attendee/Instructor Introductions

BUILDING THE FRANCHISOR ORGANIZATION
- Mission Statement
- Business Plan
- Franchise Intranet
- Staffing the Franchisor Organization
- Franchise Development Functions

TRAINING YOUR FRANCHISEES
- Developing Training Programs
- Classroom vs. On The Job Training
- Classroom Topics
- On The Job Topics

PROVIDING EFFECTIVE FIELD SUPPORT
- Field Staff Training and Evaluation
- Conducting Field Visits
- Policing vs. Consulting
- Problem Franchisees
- Effecting Positive Change in Franchisees

MARKETING AS A FRANCHISOR
- Building an Effective Marketing Program
- Marketing Media
- Control and Approval of Marketing Materials
- Managing the Marketing Fund
- The Marketing Advisory Council

FRANCHISOR COMPLIANCE
- Overview of Franchise Compliance
- Implementing Your Compliance System
- Pre-Sales Compliance
- Required Documents
- Setting Up the Calendar and Filing System
- Compliance During Sales Process
- Compliance Officer Checklist and Tracking System

FRANCHISEE RELATIONS
- Franchisee Motivators
- Techniques for Good Franchisee Relations
- Importance of Balanced Relationship
- Importance of Field Representative Position
- Franchise Advisory Council
- Conflict Resolution Case Studies

Chapter **13**

What It Costs

Ray Kroc, founder of McDonald's, once said: "The only thing you need to start a business is a customer." While there is great truth in that statement, it is hardly the whole story. Many people are eager and able to buy franchises. They are your potential customers. But before you, the new franchisor, can get from Point A – having a business that will attract such people – to Point B – being in a position to find them and offer them a franchise – a good deal must happen. Identifying the things that must happen has been one of the primary purposes of this book. Another purpose has been to show you that you can't do it alone. You will need help to get your program started and get it started right. Each of the tasks involved should be done correctly the first time, to prevent doing them a second time.

Toward this end, you will have some options in the specialized field of franchise consulting. One is the individual consultant. There are some very bright individuals out there with varying degrees of experience in franchising. Trouble is, no one person can do all of the things you've been reading about. You'll also find small companies who offer to do all of these tasks, but who farm out much of the work – such as legal documents and marketing materials – to independent contractors. Some of their work product may be excellent, some not so excellent. Finally, you can select a company that provides all of the services we have described under one roof with its own employees. One of the special advantages this type of firm offers is interactive coordination of all specialists working on the project.

How much, then, will you spend to have a franchise consultant help you put together the kind of program we've been describing in these pages? A quick answer is: probably a lot less than you would spend opening another unit of whatever you have now. Indeed, that's how many companies arrive at franchising. They exhaust every means they can think of for borrowing capital or finding investors to build another company-owned unit and turn to franchising as a last resort. One of our clients, Ron Matsch, founded Discovery Zone, a place where parents could bring young children to be entertained under adult supervision. The business boomed – so much so that people came around to take pictures of his unit, then began to "knock it off." Ron had been trying to accumulate the $300,000 he would need to build a second unit, but soon realized that he had to move faster. He didn't have enough capital for that second unit, but he did have enough to franchise. Within eighteen months after we completed his franchise development program, he had sold 160 franchises at $25,000 each. Another client, Christopher Russo of Hurricane Wings in Florida, wanted to open a second unit but lacked the capital. He asked Mike Matakaetis, a successful Dunkin' Donuts franchisee, for the financing that would enable him to open a few more. Mike suggested instead that Chris franchise Hurricane Wings. In the first six months after they were in a position to sell franchises they sold 60, and within a year had sold a total of 180. True, these are exceptional cases. As we have mentioned, the average number of first-year sales for a new franchisor is closer to ten. But with franchising the potential is always there. What is the first-year growth potential of adding one new company-owned unit? Answer: one unit.

So when you think about the cost of franchising your business think first about the risk versus potential reward. Then think about all the things we've talked about that need to be done if you're going to do it right. And finally, think about how many of those things you need to do even if you don't franchise. You know, down deep, that you really should have a Business Plan – a road map that tells where you are going, how you intend to get there, and what your expectations should be in sales, costs and profits. You know you would really like to have everything you do documented into a manual – even if it's only to be used by employees. Clients have told us again and again that one of the best things that came out of their franchise program was the tightening up, smoothing out, general consulting, manuals and Business Plan. So, while these elements are going to be part of the cost of becoming a franchisor, they are important to address, even if you don't franchise.

Let's summarize, then, all of the steps you and your consultant will need to take to put together a thoroughly comprehensive franchise program. Then we'll talk about the cost of such a program.

1. Initial Client Meeting

You will meet at the consultant's offices with department heads and individuals assigned to the project in each of the required specialties. You will describe your company and its history as well as your strategy for franchising to the extent that you have formulated it. You'll meet later with members of individual departments to discuss in detail issues related to their particular specialties and work products. A preliminary schedule for completion of work product will be established.

2. Concept Research and Review

The consultant's personnel will examine and evaluate the basic concept, operational format, and general marketing characteristics of your business, comparing them with those of similar franchisors and with comparable business models in other franchise industries. This review will encompass types of products and services offered; types and size of locations utilized; total investment for establishing an outlet; and sales and earnings of the corporate entity and franchising concept. An assessment will be made concerning their overall effect upon your franchise program.

3. Senior Consultant On-Site Analysis

A senior consultant will visit your business to review its operational characteristics and recommend policies and procedures, aimed at enhancing the franchise program. A senior consultant will also identify operational elements of the business critical to the legal, operations, and marketing aspects of the franchise program, and relay this information to appropriate personnel.

4. Franchise Structure

The consulting firm will make recommendations relating to the critical business decisions that become the foundation of the franchise program and that are incorporated into the legal, operations, and marketing documents and strategies. These issues include policy formulation, market potential, speed of expansion, the franchise structure best suited to your situation, and current company resources available to meet your franchise goals.

A. Franchise Owner Profile

Qualifications, such as financial resources, previous experience, and business skills, will be addressed, based on your needs and the consultant's knowledge of the franchise marketplace.

B. Type of Franchise Offered

Depending upon such factors as unit investment, complexity of operation, cost and nature of support programs, and expansion goals, the consultant will suggest a program to acquire individual franchises, multi-unit franchises, or subfranchises – or all three.

C. Determination of Territory

After evaluating the nature of your business, competition and other factors, the consultant will suggest whether or not the franchisee needs an exclusive territory and the degree of exclusivity. If it does, the consultant will analyze available territorial and demographic data of your existing business and prioritize appropriate criteria, such as population, competition, income levels, size of the market needed to support a franchise, industrial base, or business base.

D. Franchise Support Programs

The consultant will identify and recommend the type and scope of services to be provided to franchisees, including initial training, supervisory visits, site selection, and advertising support. In this manner, a comprehensive support program can be planned and the cost of that program anticipated.

E. Internal Staffing

The consultant will assess human resource needs for implementing your franchise program and will determine how best to meet those needs, whether by expanding the roles of current staff members, or by creating new positions. The consultant will also review your organization structure, assess its adaptability to franchising, and recommend changes, if necessary.

5. Franchise Revenue Sources

The consultant will review your revenue options and recommend appropriate revenue sources that may contribute to your income and profits. Among the available revenue sources are the following:

- **Initial Franchise Fees**
  Franchise fees will be determined after weighing various factors, among them the marketability of the franchise at various price levels, competition from other business opportunities available to potential buyers, and the cash flow produced by the business. The recommended initial franchise fee will be structured in light of a number of factors, such as front-end selling expenses, advertising, commissions, training, site and start-up assistance costs, market needs, and other variables.

- **Royalties**
  Royalties will be recommended in light of your needs and current industry practices. They will be based on the need to maintain sufficient corporate cash flow, to support general and administrative costs and franchise services, and to provide ongoing income for the continuing operation of the franchise. They must also be affordable for franchisees.

- **Advertising Fees**
  Local, cooperative, and corporate advertising fees will be recommended after an evaluation of the amounts currently spent for advertising by operating units and the type of advertising needed at the unit level. Corporate advertising fees required of franchisees will be based on the need for finished advertisements in their various forms.

- **Other**
  Some franchisors derive income from other sources as well, including the sale of products and services, leasing of assets and real property, and financing. The consultant will assist you in determining which sources are appropriate and practical.

6. Franchise Business Plan

Following the senior consultant's analysis, team members assigned to your project will review all critical decisions and weigh the impact of these decisions on key aspects of the franchise program. The consultant will complete detailed pro formas and financial projections, including a five-year cash flow analysis of individual operating units and the franchisor organization. In addition, the consultant will make final recommendations relating to the business, legal, and marketing characteristics that impact on the success of the franchise program. Finally, the consultant will formalize its recommendations into a Franchise Business Plan. This plan provides key franchise business decisions, assumptions, and financial projections needed to set short and long term goals. You can use this plan in presentations to financial institutions or for corporate planning.

FRANCHISE DOCUMENTS

7. Individual Franchise Agreement
The consultant will draft and submit to your attorney for review and approval a Franchise Agreement defining the contractual relationship between the franchisor and the franchisee. This Agreement will be developed in conjunction with input received from the consultant's program analysis and recommendations, and will be based on current industry practice and recent developments in franchise law.

8. Disclosure Document
The consultant will draft and submit to your attorney for review and approval the Disclosure Document required by the Federal Trade Commission and state regulatory agencies. This document will contain required information, arranged in the format stipulated by UFDD guidelines.

9. Franchise Registrations and Filings
After your attorney has approved the final drafts of the Franchise Agreement and Disclosure Document, the consultant will prepare the franchise registration applications required by various state regulatory agencies. Applications will be based on information provided by you and will be submitted to the your attorney for review and approval. Included in these applications are

materials such as the Uniform Franchise Registration Application, Supplemental Information Form, Salesman Disclosure Form, Uniform Consent to Service of Process, and Corporate Acknowledgment and Certification Page, as well as copies of advertising materials and the Disclosure Document. Applications will be prepared and processed for registration and/or filing states.

OPERATIONS SERVICES

10. Initial Analysis and Outline
The consultant will develop a preliminary outline that identifies and describes the topics that should be covered in the comprehensive Franchise Operations Manual. Based on discussion at the initial client meeting and material you have supplied, this outline will reflect the consultant's initial understanding of the issues relevant to the franchisee and will be specifically tailored to the franchise concept. It will also indicate the points at which the manual should cross-reference the provisions of the Franchise Agreement and will delineate the areas for which systems must be developed to monitor the operations of the franchisee. The outline is designed to aid the process of implementing the franchise program and will further serve as the agenda for the field visit by the operations consultant.

11. On Site Analysis and Consulting
An operations consultant will visit your place of business to observe its operations first-hand and to discuss the preliminary outline. Subject to your approval, the consultant will determine the manual's style, scope, and

format, and will document procedures, collecting any materials that are to be included in the manual.

12. Franchise Operations Manual

The Operations Department will create a customized, comprehensive manual incorporating information essential to the operation of the franchise. Its content will be based on data obtained in meetings with you, the observation of the business, the final franchise documents prepared for the program, as well as the consultant's extensive experience.

ADVERTISING AND MARKETING SERVICES

13. The Franchise Marketing Plan

The consultant will develop a comprehensive plan for generating franchise sales leads. This plan will recommend specific marketing activities and will include appropriate creative materials – such as direct mail letters and copy and layout for franchise sales ads – that can be utilized in the franchise sales campaign. The Marketing Plan will incorporate specific media suggestions, a budget for the campaign, and a timetable for implementation. It will also contain useful information on topics such as legal constraints on franchise marketing, how to obtain publicity, how to make best use of the Internet, and whether to conduct seminars and participate in trade shows. Copy for the ad and letter will be developed within the context of the consultant's experience, with guidelines established by the Federal Trade Commission, and by various state regulatory agencies whose approval is required before any advertising materials can be used in connection with the offer of a franchise.

14. Internet Marketing

Because of the extraordinary impact of the Internet on franchise marketing, the consultant will provide instruction and recommendations on how to make effective use of this new advertising medium.

15. Franchise Brochure

The consultant will develop copy and layout for a four-color brochure of approximately six to twelve pages, plus cover, designed to describe your franchise and to build enthusiasm among prospective franchisees. The brochure will describe in detail the distinctiveness of the concept, the benefits of the franchise program, and the market for its products and/or services. The consultant will provide a DVD/CD-ROM containing the franchise brochure layout.

FRANCHISE SALES TRAINING AND SUPPORT

16. Franchise Sales Training

The consultant will provide a Franchise Sales Training course for you and your sales personnel. The course includes a comprehensive overview of the franchise sales process, plus detailed instruction in proven franchise sales techniques, proper lead follow-up procedures, including Internet lead tracking, state and federal legal requirements pertaining to franchise sales, and franchise trade shows and sales seminar presentations.

17. Franchise Sales Manual

Each person attending sales training should receive a franchise sales manual for use as a reference guide, and as a textbook for instructing franchise sales personnel. The manual should provide useful information on all aspects of the franchise sales process, including the psychology of the franchise buyer, complying with federal and state franchise disclosure laws, establishing a lead-tracking system, showing your facility to its best advantage, and conveying the benefits of franchising. Also included should be information on how to conduct seminars, hold an open house, work trade shows, plus sections on special franchising situations, including area development, and master and conversion franchises.

18. Franchise Sales Implementation

The consultant will be available for hands-on assistance in your franchise sales process. This critical support can include preliminary trade show training, in-show consulting and guidance, sales presentations and follow-up meetings with prospective buyers, reviewing your sales techniques, coaching sales staff, and guidance in establishing proper methods of their franchise sales presentations.

FRANCHISE MANAGEMENT TRAINING

19. Franchise Management Training

The consultant should offer a Franchise Management Training course designed to educate the client's management team on the complexities of operating and managing a growing franchise organization. Detailed and comprehensive manuals should be provided to all attendees on all course segments. Topics include:

A. Building The Franchise Organization
Discusses key development issues that franchise companies need to address as they expand their business systems.

B. Training Your Franchisees
Recommends procedures for building a comprehensive training program. It also encompasses relevant issues such as management and operation of the franchise business, preparation of products or services, quality assurance, personnel management, advertising, bookkeeping, use of trademarks, maintenance of trade secrets, legal obligations, customer relations, operational requirements and other issues.

C. Providing Effective Field Support
Suggests guidelines for hiring field support personnel, for establishing field support procedures and for evaluating the standards of each franchise at the unit level.

D. Marketing as a Franchisor
Discusses the importance of creating a marketing program to assist franchisees in building sales and in gaining market recognition.

E. Franchisor Compliance
Covers the necessary steps for understanding and implementing federal and state compliance requirements.

F. Franchisee Relations
The issues in this segment go beyond the technical obligations articulated in the Franchise Agreement. They address many of the ways in which the franchisor can create a positive, long-term business relationship with its franchisees, which are essential to the success of the franchise.

GENERAL CONSULTING

20. One-Year General Consulting
For the first year after taking on the project, a responsible consultant will be available to advise and assist in the implementation of the Client's franchise program and to supply useful information concerning current practices in the industry and in franchising in general.

If this sounds like a lot of work, it is. Generally speaking, the entire project should take about six to eight months and should cost between $100,000 and $150,000. But your expenses don't end there. You'll need outside legal help and an audit for your new corporation. You'll also need funds to print your brochure and Operations Manual, to advertise for franchisees, for travel and for working expenses. If you plan to file in registration states, there are individual filing fees for each state. All told, you're probably looking at another $30,000 to $60,000 for these items. Of course, a reputable consultant will probably allow you to pay by installments over a one-year period. In addition, some of your costs (such as franchise advertising) will not kick in until the program itself is completed and necessary state registrations have been filed—probably in the ninth, tenth or eleventh month.

We have done our best not to sugarcoat the cost issue. We believe this to be a realistic assessment of what you'll need, what it will cost, and how long it will take. Can you build another company-owned unit for this amount? And even if you can will you be likely to lose money the first year with a manager running it, break even the second year, and really not make any money until the third year? View that scenario against selling just ten franchises the first year at $40,000 each and thereby collecting $400,000 against minimal costs. Remember, the franchisee pays you a franchise fee of $35,000 to $50,000, puts up all the money to build and operate the unit, comes to work for you in training for one to two months and pays you a royalty of 4 to 10 percent of sales. Even companies like McDonald's, Kentucky Fried Chicken, Taco Bell and Pizza Hut are selling off company-owned units to recoup their cash, eliminate the day-to-day management headaches and permit more rapid expansion. Think about it!

Going International

For most new franchisors, international franchising (other than Canada) is a distant dream. Building a strong domestic program is far and away the most important goal. But for a few new franchisors the prospect of expansion beyond US borders may be, if not imminent, foreseeable. Such companies are of two general types. Already large businesses that are simply employing franchising as one of several growth strategies may be positioned to expand internationally as soon as the franchise program is up and running. Then there are businesses with concepts so alluring to consumers that foreign as well as domestic buyers come flocking. If your business is one of these, the following remarks about international franchising may be useful in the near future. If not, they may come in handy down the road.

* * *

Globalization, as we all know, is both good and bad news. US companies grow by expanding internationally and American consumers benefit by enjoying low prices on imported goods. That's the good news. Meanwhile, American workers are laid off and US exports decline. That's the bad news.

There is one aspect of globalization, however, that so far seems nothing but good news for all concerned – when it works right. That aspect is international franchising. When American franchisors sell licenses abroad they improve the balance of trade and they bring revenue home to owners and stockholders. Because the "product" they are exporting is intellectual property – their name and system of doing business – there are no tariffs to be paid and no American jobs are lost. The same is basically true of any country that franchises across its borders.

International franchising is the process whereby a franchisor in one country sells a license to operate the franchisor's business to a company or individual in another country. Typically, these licenses are for master franchises consisting of a specific number of units in a large geographical area – sometimes an entire country. Rarely are the licenses for a single unit. Indeed, "license" is the word of choice internationally because laws pertaining specifically to franchising are found primarily in the United States.

US franchisors were selling licenses overseas as early as the 1930s when Wimpy's, a Chicago hamburger chain, found a buyer in the UK. Wimpy's became so popular there that Wimpy became the generic name for hamburger, much as Formica at one time became the generic name for all plastic laminates. In those days, Coca Cola sold bottling company franchises overseas as well.

World War II brought international franchising to a virtual stop, and not until the 1960s did it resume to any degree. In fact, the first great business format franchisor, McDonald's, became the first great international franchisor. Not that it wasn't a struggle. McDonald's first international venture in 1965 involved the sale of the rights to develop the Caribbean to two Americans. Unfortunately, McDonald's made mistakes in structuring the deal, and although thirty units were established they were poorly operated and eventually failed. Two years later McDonald's sold franchise territories in Canada and the Netherlands, but both entities struggled in the early going. The company's first overseas success came in Japan, where McDonald's in 1971 formed a 50-50 joint venture with Den Fujita, founder and owner of a Japanese import company. By 1983 revenues from McDonald's Japan exceeded those of the country's largest native restaurant chain. Growth overseas continued, and by 1992 McDonald's units outside the United States were generating $8.6 billion in food sales or fully 39 percent of its $21.9 billion in worldwide system sales. Nor was McDonald's the only overseas franchisor. US hotel chains and auto rental agencies became especially prominent internationally.

Our company, Francorp, became involved in international franchising early on. In 1976 we were invited by Jollibee, a four-unit hamburger restaurant chain in the Philippines, to help them franchise through-out the Philippines. Much later we assisted their entry into the United States. By 2007 they had 500 units in the Philippines – more than McDonald's – and twelve in the US. What spurred their success? Tony Tan Oak-tong, chairman of Jollibee, positioned his company as the Philippine version of the American fast food restaurant, a la McDonald's. He recognized before many others that some aspects of American culture are highly marketable to people outside the United States. Even McDonald's had trouble learning that lesson. When they first entered China they tried to compete there the way they have done in the US, on the basis of price. But "buy one – get one free" was, in our opinion, a futile gesture in competition with low-priced Chinese restaurants. When McDonald's extended their hours and upgraded décor, sales increased by 11 percent.

Today the recognition of culture as a commodity is more common. In China, Haagen Dazs ice cream that sells for $1 in the US costs $4.00. A cup of Starbucks coffee costs three times as much there as it does here. At Pizza Hut pizza goes for $10 a slice. Companies like Hard Rock Café and TGIF are successful abroad not so much because of their cuisine as their cachet. Ning Wen, a Chinese importer/exporter, said to us, "Chinese people don't go to Pizza Hut for the pizza. They don't particularly like pizza. They go there for the culture!"

As all of this suggests, going international is not a step to be taken lightly – especially by companies new to franchising. Pitfalls are plentiful. Here are a few:

- **Large fees.**
  A problem? You bet. It may be possible to
  sell a territory for several hundreds of
  thousands of dollars. But unless you've
  calculated the costs of training, support, and
  international travel (airfare, hotels, rental
  cars, living expenses, salaries) very carefully,
  you may find you have a new international
  licensee but little to show for it. This is
  especially true in countries where the dollar
  is weak. Economists estimate that the dollar
  will continue to decline against the euro
  through 2010 – perhaps by as much as
  40 percent. This means, of course, that whatever franchise fee you seek may be considered
  a bargain in countries that employ the euro,
  but in those countries you must be especially
  careful when assessing your support
  expenditures. The same is true for Canada,
  Australia, New Zealand. On the other hand,
  your franchise may be perceived as expensive
  in countries like Egypt, China, Thailand and
  South Africa, where local currencies are still
  weak against the dollar. There, living costs for
  your support staff will be relatively low.
  　　This said, you should know that traditionally European countries are less inclined to pay
  large up-front fees for franchise rights.

They typically want to open a single unit, operate it for two years, then decide whether or not to commit to a more aggressive development schedule. For this reason, fewer US companies do deals in the European countries than elsewhere. In Asia and the Mideast, and to a lesser degree Latin America, it is far more common for companies to pay larger up-front fees and agree to aggressive expansion schedules. In our view, Asia, particularly China, is the most fertile market for international franchising.

- **The market and the culture**.
  Consider Japan. Its economic base is second only to that of the United States. On the one hand the population is large – about 150 million or half the population of the United States. On the other hand, the country's land mass is small. Japan would fit easily into the state of California! Yet 76 percent of Japan is uninhabitable! Fifty-two percent of Japan's population is located in a 300-mile corridor between Tokyo and Osaka! Talk about population density! It's an area made in heaven for businesses. Knowing facts like these can be extremely helpful in establishing a franchise there. But that's not all you need to know. There's the Japanese culture to be considered. Since 1980, Francorp has worked closely with Roy Fujita, a valued partner in our Francorp Japan operation who has been bringing US companies to Japan and Japanese companies to the US. Our experience has been that if you sell

the rights to your franchise for all of Japan, and the buyer is located in Tokyo, that franchisee may never venture out of the Tokyo market. For this reason, if you go franchising in Japan you will either want to establish strict performance requirements or sell only the rights to Tokyo, perhaps with options on other cities.

• **Your name.**
If you've chosen a country where the native language is not English, be sure that the name of your business in translation is acceptable (or be willing to change it for that country).

• **Taxes.**
Japan takes 10 percent in taxes on all royalties going out of the country. You will also pay US taxes. If your royalty is 5 percent and Japan takes .5 percent and the US takes .5 percent, that leaves you with 4% percent. Will the deal work at 4 percent? Be sure of your pricing strategy before you sign.

• **Laws.**
Copyright and trademark laws vary from country to country. Others put up ownership and other barriers. Until 2007 China required that foreign companies establish company-owned operations for two years before selling franchises. Brazil has been a problem for foreign franchisors. A Brazilian firm sought the rights to open a Francorp franchise consulting franchise in Brazil. We turned them down because we felt they lacked proper qualifications. They opened a bogus "Francorp

Brazil" office anyway, and we spent twelve years trying to get a trademark infringement case heard in Brazilian courts—unsuccessfully.

- **Buyers.**
  Some who have plenty of capital may have no qualifications for operating the business. Investigate first.

With these issues in mind, let's look at what we believe to be the most effective, most profitable way for two parties, US and foreign, or any franchisor and franchisee in different countries, to structure a deal that will work to everyone's satisfaction.

An eight-step international checklist

1. **Are you ready?**
   Do you have the operational organization to establish and support foreign operations?

2. **Know your market**
   You will need to do some homework to determine if your concept is adaptable in the licensee's country and find out what adjustments you and they will need to make. Learn about their culture, geography, demographics, monetary system, and business practices.

3. **Pick the right partner**
   Because your licensee will be a multi-unit buyer, it's even more critical than in selling individual franchises to choose correctly.

Don't sell to anyone unless they are financially and operationally capable of developing the region you are selling. This almost certainly means someone already doing business in that country.

4. Price it fairly

Over-price and you may lose a buyer. Under-price and you will lose money. Structure the deal so that you receive enough up front to cover commissions, referral fees (if any), market studies, extensive and intensive training, travel expenses for the first two years, and the necessary support costs. Three components are involved: 1) the initial fee, 2) royalties, and 3) out of pocket expenses.

5. Require performance

Be sure to set specific numbers of units and target dates. A requisite number of units should be opened in each major city each year, or the license rights subject to termination.

6. Provide support

The higher the quality-control sensitivity your business, the more support, monitoring and visibility you will need to commit. Time and distance further complicate this issue. Before you finalize the pricing of your fees and royalties, be sure you have adequately evaluated the level of support, costs and involvement you will need to commit to the success of international licenses.

7. **Develop product sources**

   If your international franchisees will need merchandise, equipment or products in the operation of their businesses, be sure that those products are available in their country at prices that are affordable and do not adversely affect unit economics. If they have to import your products or others', you need to evaluate and factor in the tariffs or barriers to entry of these products and often help locate them and negotiate with suppliers.

8. **Make your program win-win-win**

   Your main objective in foreign markets is to create a fair and equitable, long-lasting business relationship in which everyone benefits – the consumer, the international licensee, and your company. It must work at all levels.

If your business is successful and has franchising potential, it's quite possible that a foreign company will contact you about obtaining a license. If you are relatively small and new to franchising, beware. Don't let the prospect of a big fee allow you to take a step you are not prepared for. Even large companies have blundered into foreign markets with disastrous results. KFC floundered on its initial entry into Japan and Hong Kong; Jack-in-the-Box had problems in Asia; Radio Shack lost $35 million in Japan; and many other US companies collected large up-front fees only to watch some of these foreign operations fail. If you are approached, make an objective appraisal of your readiness by using the checklist given above.

Typically, when selling license rights to foreign companies, those companies will intend to open and operate the units themselves, not franchise them to others. Mitsubishi and Mitsui operate a number of US franchises in Japan. They do not sell franchises. You may also be surprised that your foreign buyer does not focus on unit economics – that is, how profitable your stores or restaurants are. They are more interested in whether or not your concept will appeal to people in their countries. Again as Ning Wen, our Chinese consultant friend, points out, foreign buyers are buying the culture, not the product, for many US and Western concepts. You should also be aware that Asians, and particularly the Japanese, take a long-term view on developing businesses. In the US, if we start a business and it doesn't do well in a relatively short period of time, we frequently pull the plug. The Japanese have a great deal more patience and are prepared to nurture and develop the business to profitability.

Franchising works well in foreign countries for the very reasons they want to buy them. Lacking our US maverick, entrepreneurial tendencies, they have fewer new business concepts of their own. On the other hand, many foreigners tend to be comfortable – even eager – to follow rules and formats that are clearly delineated. Mr. Donut was a second tier player in the US. They sold the rights to Japan to Duskin, a partly owned subsidiary of Mitsui, which has an outstanding training facility, practically a replication of McDonald's Hamburger University. We were highly impressed when visiting the Mr. Donut units in Japan. They were clean, well stocked, well staffed, their products were beautifully displayed, and two attractively uniformed young ladies bowed as we entered. The tables were made of butcher block and everything was spotless. Mr. Donut operations in Japan became far superior to those in the US because of Duskin's strong training and implementation, as well as operational commitment and support.

One of the first steps you should take after selling a license in a foreign country is to engage a consultant in that country, at your licensee's expense, to create a Marketing and Business Development Plan. While you will be a participant in the process, the burden of doing the research should fall on your licensee. You are in no position to identify and assess country, province or municipal rules and regulations, local property or rental costs, advertising rates, traffic patterns, regional differences, competitive environment, demographics, etc. You should provide your licensee with the template of required information and assist and guide them in the process. Generally, you will charge a one-time fee, say $200,000 to $500,000, plus $1,000 to $10,000 for every unit they open or franchise, plus a royalty of 1 percent to 5 percent, depending on how often you will need to go there and what ongoing support you will need to provide. Also take into account whether or not you will be selling them products. We strongly advise, in addition to whatever fee you charge up front, that you build into the contract all out-of-pocket costs for the first two years, over and above royalties. We wish we could give you an exact formula for calculating the price for a country, but there are too many variables. A market of one million people may be ideal for forty fast-food outlets but only one temporary office placement company. In truth, it often becomes as unscientific as "what the market will bear."

If anything, franchising is an even better way to expand into other countries than in one's own. It places full responsibility for the success of the enterprise upon the licensee, who is far better qualified to deal with the culture, language, monetary system, laws, hiring practices, marketing methods, product sources, and real estate than you are. But be careful. One false step can doom your prospects for many years to come. On the other hand, one successful licensee can lead to incredible growth worldwide. Good luck!

Chapter 15

Trends Worth Watching

Well, let's assume your franchise is up and running, franchisees are coming into the fold, and the future looks altogether rosy. It's happened to many others before you, so it's not really a great stretch. You've been in business long enough, however, to know that there are no guarantees. Roadblocks can appear at any time. But the roadblocks – as well as the opportunities – that confront a relatively small entrepreneur are often quite different from those that confront a franchisor with a growing regional, national or even international chain. In that capacity, you will need to broaden your vision, to look beyond the immediate and to be aware of trends in franchising that might effect you and everyone in your burgeoning organization.

In one respect you can be relatively confident. Franchising itself will continue to prosper. Since 1954, when McDonald's gave business format franchising a rocket-size boost, the National Bureau of Economic

Research identifies eight recessions in the United States: one in the Fifties, two in the Sixties, one in the Seventies, two in the Eighties, one in the Nineties, and the most recent in 2001. Throughout that period the number of franchisors and franchisees has continued to grow. It's our belief, in fact, that recessions are almost as good for franchising as economic booms.

There are two reasons for this puzzling phenomenon. One has to do with the nature of franchising itself. Franchising is not an industry. It is an expansion strategy that can be used by any industry, indeed by any business. So a slump in any one industry will have relatively little effect upon franchising as a whole. But recessions, you may argue, affect all industries. That brings us to the second reason. It has to do with the way most franchises are financed: with home equity. Median home prices in the United States, according to the National Association of Realtors, rose from $20,000 in 1968 to $185,000 in 2004. Even after the housing bust of 2005 through 2008, homes remain for many people gigantic savings accounts, that can be tapped by both franchisors and franchisees. Entrepreneurs tap them to start new businesses and in some cases franchise them. Franchisees tap them to buy franchises. So when the economy is good, the average person who wants to own a business decides it might be the right time to buy a franchise, which has come to be regarded as the investment with a safety net. And his or her home equity makes it possible. When times are tough, people who are the victims of layoffs, downsizing, re-engineering, mergers, and acquisitions also decide it might be the time to buy a franchise. In the past, many such people who thought about owning their own business were afraid to quit their jobs and take on the risk. Once the decision is made for them, in the form of a severance notice, and after what in some cases is a prolonged job search, they explore the possibility of owning their own business. They, too, realize that franchising represents an investment with a safety net. And their home equity makes it possible also.

The bottom line is that as long as people have new business concepts or ways to improve existing concepts and as long as people want to expand their businesses but are impeded by lack of capital, the need for qualified and dedicated staff, and the desire to move faster than their present system will allow, there will be an ongoing and endless supply of companies that want to franchise. As long as people want to own their own businesses, be their own boss, enjoy the benefits that a franchise relationship provides with lower risk, there will be buyers. Recession or no recession.

Incidentally, we have noticed yet another trend among people who buy franchises. Young people who prefer not to work for someone else solicit capital to start a business from family members. Family members, in turn, suggest a franchise as a way of maximizing the chance that the young person will succeed. At the other end of the spectrum, people in their forties, fifties and even sixties buy franchises (1) to earn money for retirement or (2) because having reached retirement they want something productive to do.

One trend we have observed in recent years is the tendency for medium and even large companies to turn to franchising. And they do so for some of the same reasons that smaller companies turn to franchising: to saturate a market quickly or because cash is limited. At an investment of $1 million each, it would cost McDonald's, Burger King and Wendy's $100 million to open 100 new restaurants, a target they have exceeded annually for many years. But even companies of their size don't have that kind of cash available in their checkbooks. Yet they know that they are in hand-to-hand combat for market share. So they continue to franchise. As we noted earlier, Krystal Hamburgers had 400 company-owned units before it started franchising. Allstate Insurance only started franchising in recent years, well after they had established national presence with company-owned offices.

Some companies that are strong in one or more regions franchise in new markets because it would take too long to establish company-owned units there, to say nothing about the capital needed. When Yum!, the buyer of KFC, Taco Bell, and Pizza Hut, went public, even the money they raised wasn't enough to execute their expansion strategy. They sold off company-owned units as franchises to create cash for the company's infrastructure and expansion. Another Yum! initiative that has become a trend is dual and triple branding. Yum! is combining Pizza Hut, KFC and Taco Bell under one roof – with one manager, common seating and one kitchen in one building on one piece of land. It's a great way to reduce costs and attract a family with diverse appetites. Dunkin' Donuts has congregated Togo's, a sandwich operation, and Baskin Robbins ice cream in one unit. The three separate businesses attract customers throughout the day. Auto malls have appeared on the landscape, combining muffler shops, brake shops, auto accessory stores, car washes, and auto stereo shops into one location.

More and more multiple unit franchises are being sold, as better-capitalized and more sophisticated buyers are surfacing who are investor-managers with the talent for running large operations. They, in turn, can franchise or operate company-owned units or both. More capital has become available to the franchising sector in general – for franchisors and franchisees. Investors have gained more confidence in investing in franchising because of the lower likelihood of failure.

We will see more conversion franchising as various fragmented industries, composed of independent businesses, need to combine to compete against the market power of large companies, just as Century 21, Red Carpet, and Coldwell Banker gathered together independent real estate brokers under nationally known identities. Small service businesses, chiropractors, dry cleaners, bars, attorneys, accountants, tax preparers, check cashing, convenience stores, coffee shops, carpet cleaners, lawn care, handymen, and other fragmented industries are eligible for conversion franchising. It's just a matter of time, necessity, opportunity, and vision until someone does it. The impact of the Internet on franchising, already huge, will continue to grow. Search engine optimization, ads that drive people to your Internet site, Internet ad campaigns, email marketing, Intranet connection of brick and mortar operations with e-commerce sites, such as The Sharper Image has done – these will all be part of the application of the Internet as they apply to franchising. Anyone who doesn't learn how to effectively harness the power of the Internet won't be around very long.

More franchise companies will continue to be acquired by large companies. We saw this early on when KFC, Taco Bell, and Pizza Hut were acquired by Pepsi Cola, when Service Master acquired Terminex, Cendant acquired Century 21 and Coldwell Banker. But we've also seen it on a smaller scale with companies like the Dwyer Group which acquired several very small companies and with their knowledge, experience, and expertise in franchising built them into larger entities. Neal Aaronson, a franchise veteran, formed a company to acquire Cinnabon, Carvel, and several other brands. There's much more to come in this area, and some new franchisors as they become successful can expect buy-out offers.

International franchising is bringing nations closer together. More and more companies all over the world are expanding into other countries. Studies done by Francorp in 2006 suggest that more than 20,000 franchisors in 48 countries have annual sales exceeding $1.6 trillion. Wall Street loves franchising too. A number of franchising companies have paved the way by being top performers in the stock market. If you had bought 100 shares of McDonald's stock for $2250 when it went public in 1965 and held them until December 29, 2006 their value after seven stock splits would have been approximately $3.3 million. Wall Street knows it and so do investors. There is a great market opportunity for good franchise companies that want to go public.

More financial companies will continue to target the franchise industry. The trend in the past has been vertical – that is, financial companies seeking to do business with franchisors or franchisees usually have specialized in one type of financing – i.e. real estate, or equipment, or receivables, or investing in furniture or working capital. The trend now is, and increasingly will be, financial groups that "bundle" all of a franchisor's needs into one package on the lending side. There is also an increasing trend among venture capital groups to infuse capital in franchise companies that enables them to grow rapidly to the point that a public offering can be made. Blockbuster, Discovery Zone and Boston Market are examples.

If we had to pick a single trend that will exceed all others in its impact upon franchising, it has to be the Internet. The Internet has already changed the way we sell franchises. As time goes on it will increasingly become the Battlefield for Franchise Sales.

Chapter 16

Considering The Possibilities

Let's go back a minute to where we were at the beginning of the last chapter. You are selling franchises. Some franchisees are already in business. Others soon will be. What next?

At this point it will be worth thinking about where your franchise program may lead. What are the long-term possibilities you should be considering? We can suggest four of them once you have put a comprehensive, efficient franchise program in place and have demonstrated (1) that people are interested in buying your franchise and (2) that, having bought it, are operating their own units profitably.

The first possibility is the one that most people dream of when they first start franchising. Their franchise will grow to become a regional, national and even international player in their field. Their corporation will grow accordingly, eventually go public and operate hundreds or thousands of units around the world. However, in all candor, the likelihood of such extraordinary success is not high. As we noted earlier, only 5% of franchises have 500 locations or more. And many of these first appeared in the vanguard of franchising back in the Fifties, Sixties and Seventies. Even McDonald's didn't become a giant overnight. Still, the goal is by no means impossible. Auntie Anne's Pretzels, a company we helped become a franchisor in the 1980s, now has nearly a thousand units worldwide.

Possiblity #2 is a limited version of #1. Your franchise grows to a level where either the market or – more likely – your own ambition causes a slowdown in its growth rate. That doesn't necessarily mean there are problems. Outlets are successful. Royalties are coming in. Franchises continue to be sold. But your comfort level has increased over the years and the burning ambition that made your program successful at the beginning perhaps isn't as intense as it used to be. Hardly surprising, and nothing to apologize for. Hundreds of franchises today are highly successful without being giants, including many of our clients: USA Baby (60 units at this writing), Champion Cleaners (70 units), Damon's Grill (100 units), Jersey Mike's (250 units), Nix Check Cashing (60 units), PIP Printing (400 units). The list goes on and on.

One down-the-road strategy that few franchisors consider at the beginning is the franchisee buyout. Franchising is attractive to entrepreneurs, as we have stressed over and over again, because it can generate capital for growth not available elsewhere. But supposing a company's capital problems have been solved? What if the franchise grows so briskly that it attracts not only franchisees and customers but prospective investors. The next step can be to go public and use the funds raised to buy out franchises and convert them to company-owned units. Ruth's Chris Steak House, the high end restaurant chain, did just that. But, you ask, don't franchises typically outperform company-owned units? Sure, but if you can afford it would you rather get a 6 percent royalty from a franchise generating $1,000,000 in sales per year or own a restaurant generating $800,000 a year and get 100 percent of the profits, plus whatever tax advantages that might accrue?

Possibility #4 is a more obvious one. You can build your franchise to a respectable size, then sell it. At least once a month we get calls from venture capitalists, hedge fund managers and other investors eager to buy a growing franchise. Why? Because franchisors get royalty income, and royalty income represents a steady revenue stream. After all, any franchisee can have a bad year. Sales drop from, say, $600,000 to $400,000. The franchisee may even lose money in that year. But the franchisor's revenue stream merely dwindles (at 6 percent royalty) from $36,000 to $24,000. *Quel dommage!* And that's not all. Investors find that franchises are relatively easy to evaluate because their financial statements tend to be accurate. Growth in sales and in units are measurable and, to some degree, predictable, based upon past performance. One of our clients, Discovery Zone, achieved a market value of nearly $900 million after five years. It was later sold to Blockbuster. Another, Hair Performers, grew to more than 250 units before being sold. And, by the way, the aforementioned Auntie Anne's was sold by its founder in 2005 for $250 million. In contrast, selling a business that you own entirely is not always easy. We know a man whose restaurant generated $500,000 in sales annually. For personal reasons, he found it necessary to sell. The best he could get was $80,000, or barely the amount of the physical assets – kitchen equipment, tables and chairs, etc. – of the business.

If any of these possibilities become actualities, congratulations! All are indicative of true success in franchising.

Conclusion

They say we're in the Information Age and that information is power. Well, we've shared with you a fair amount of information, but the question is: What are you going to do with it? If you are in the process of considering franchising, then we hope we've helped you in the decision-making process. If you're a client, or are already franchising, we know that you and, more importantly, your employees, present, and future, will find this information useful. Use this book as a primer for your new people, a supplement or refresher to what you may have already been exposed to, and a reference source for new problems, opportunities, and challenges.

We have worked with a wide range of clients, from small embryonic idea stages to some of the largest companies in the world, like McDonald's, Nestle, Holiday Inn, BPH, Blockbuster, Ace Hardware, KFC, Ryder Trucks, and many others. Many of these and other companies operate from the same informational base. If you were to obtain a copy of their operations manuals, KFC's secret formula for fried chicken, or all of their computer information, you would still not be guaranteed to succeed. The real power is not in the information – it's in you! You are the key to the success of your company. It can never rise above the level of your intensity, commitment, knowledge, quality of your decisions, work ethic, and most importantly, vision.

Lastly, as a reminder of what determination can do, let us tell you about a fast food franchisor of our acquaintance we encountered recently. We asked him how things were going and he said that since 1987 when we helped him launch his franchise program his company had grown from one unit to 800 and that he was continuing to open an average of one new franchise a week. "Looking back," he said, "I wasn't confident that we would sell one franchise. I didn't know if we would or not. But we had to take the chance. I remember a busy Sunday afternoon. A lady came up to me in the restaurant and says to me, 'Don't ever franchise this thing. You'll ruin it.' I'll never forget that."

INDEX